Peirce

GUIDES FOR THE PERPLEXED

Guides for the Perplexed are clear, concise, and accessible introductions to thinkers, writers, and subjects that students and readers can find especially challenging. Concentrating specifically on what it is that makes the subject difficult to grasp, these books explain and explore key themes and ideas, guiding the reader toward a thorough understanding of demanding material.

Adorno: A Guide for the Perplexed, Alex Thomson
Aquinas: A Guide for the Perplexed, Pater S. Eardley and Carl N. Still
Arendt: A Guide for the Perplexed, Karin Fry
Aristotle: A Guide for the Perplexed, John Vella
Augustine: A Guide for the Perplexed, James Wetzel
Bentham: A Guide for the Perplexed, Philip Schofield
Berkeley: A Guide for the Perplexed, Talia Bettcher
Deleuze: A Guide for the Perplexed, Claire Colebrook
Derrida: A Guide for the Perplexed, Julian Wolfreys
Descartes: A Guide for the Perplexed, Justin Skirry
The Empiricists: A Guide for the Perplexed, Laurence Carlin
Existentialism: A Guide for the Perplexed, Stephen Earnshaw
Freud: A Guide for the Perplexed, Celine Surprenant
Gadamer: A Guide for the Perplexed, Chris Lawn
Habermas: A Guide for the Perplexed, Lasse Thomassen
Hegel: A Guide for the Perplexed, David James
Heidegger: A Guide for the Perplexed, David Cerbone
Hobbes: A Guide for the Perplexed, Stephen J. Finn
Hume: A Guide for the Perplexed, Angela Coventry
Husserl: A Guide for the Perplexed, Matheson Russell
Kant: A Guide for the Perplexed, TK Seung
Kierkegaard: A Guide for the Perplexed, Clare Carlisle
Leibniz: A Guide for the Perplexed, Franklin Perkins
Levinas: A Guide for the Perplexed, B. C. Hutchens
Locke: A Guide for the Perplexed, Patricia Sheridan
Marx: A Guide for the Perplexed, John Sheed

Merleau-Ponty: A Guide for the Perplexed, Eric Matthews
Nietzsche: A Guide for the Perplexed, R. Kevin Hill
Plato: A Guide for the Perplexed, Gerald A. Press
Pragmatism: A Guide for the Perplexed, Robert B. Talisse and Scott F. Aikin
Quine: A Guide for the Perplexed, Gary Kemp
Relativism: A Guide for the Perplexed, Timothy Mosteller
Ricoeur: A Guide for the Perplexed, David Pellauer
Rousseau: A Guide for the Perplexed, Matthew Simpson
Sartre: A Guide for the Perplexed, Gary Cox
Schopenhauer: A Guide for the Perplexed, R. Raj Singh
Socrates: A Guide for the Perplexed, Sara Ahbel-Rappe
Spinoza: A Guide for the Perplexed, Charles Jarrett
The Stoics: A Guide for the Perplexed, M. Andrew Holowchak
Utilitarianism: A Guide for the Perplexed, Krister Bykvist

A GUIDE FOR THE PERPLEXED

Peirce

CORNELIS DE WAAL

BLOOMSBURY
LONDON · NEW DELHI · NEW YORK · SYDNEY

Bloomsbury Academic
An imprint of Bloomsbury Publishing Plc

50 Bedford Square
London
WC1B 3DP
UK

1385 Broadway
New York
NY 10018
USA

www.bloomsbury.com

Bloomsbury is a registered trade mark of Bloomsbury Publishing Plc

First published 2013
Reprinted 2014

© Cornelis de Waal, 2013

Cornelis de Waal has asserted his right under the Copyright, Designs and Patents Act, 1988, to be identified as Author of this work.

All rights reserved. No part of this publication may be reproduced or transmitted in any form or by any means, electronic or mechanical, including photocopying, recording, or any information storage or retrieval system, without prior permission in writing from the publishers.

No responsibility for loss caused to any individual or organization acting on or refraining from action as a result of the material in this publication can be accepted by Bloomsbury or the author.

British Library Cataloguing-in-Publication Data
A catalogue record for this book is available from the British Library.

ISBN: HB: 978-1-8470-6515-5
PB: 978-1-8470-6516-2

Library of Congress Cataloging-in-Publication Data
De Waal, Cornelis.
Peirce: a guide for the perplexed/Cornelis de Waal. – First [edition].
pages cm – (Guides for the perplexed)
Includes bibliographical references and index.
ISBN 978-1-84706-515-5 (hardback) –
ISBN 978-1-84706-516-2 (paperback) –
ISBN 978-1-4411-9862-4 (ebook pdf) (print)
1. Peirce, Charles S. (Charles Sanders), 1839–1914. I. Title.
B945.P44D385 2013
191–dc23
2012020371

Typeset by Deanta Global Publishing Services, Chennai, India

*For Kelly, Livvy,
and Sophia Arisbe*

CONTENTS

Abbreviations xi

1 Life and work 1
    1.1   The birth of a polymath 3
    1.2   An outsider 6
    1.3   The Peirce papers 8
    1.4   Classifying the sciences 10

2 Mathematics and philosophy 15
    2.1   Kant's conception of mathematics 17
    2.2   The exact study of ideal states of things 20
    2.3   Mathematical reasoning 23
    2.4   Mathematics, philosophy, and logic 29

3 Phenomenology and the categories 33
    3.1   Phenomenology 34
    3.2   Derivation of the categories 39

4 The normative science of logic 47
    4.1   Grounding logic in ethics and esthetics 49
    4.2   Instinct versus reason 53
    4.3   The elementary modes of reasoning 56
    4.4   Deduction and induction 60
    4.5   Abduction 63
    4.6   The logic of relatives 66
    4.7   The geometry of thought: Existential graphs 69

5 Semeiotics, or the doctrine of signs 73
- 5.1 Two schools of semeiotics 75
- 5.2 Peirce's definition of the sign 78
- 5.3 The interpretant 81
- 5.4 The object 85
- 5.5 Three questions 87
- 5.6 A classification of signs 90

6 Philosophy of science 93
- 6.1 The sole purpose of inquiry is to fix belief 94
- 6.2 Four ways of fixing belief 96
- 6.3 The demarcation of science 102

7 Pragmatism 109
- 7.1 "How to Make Our Ideas Clear" 111
- 7.2 Proving pragmatism 116
- 7.3 Some applications of the pragmatic maxim 120

8 Truth and reality 125
- 8.1 Getting clear on truth and reality 127
- 8.2 Truth as the end of inquiry 130
- 8.3 Nominalism, realism, idealism 136

9 Mind, God, and cosmos 141
- 9.1 A critique of determinism 142
- 9.2 Three modes of evolution 144
- 9.3 The origin and nature of natural laws 148
- 9.4 Mind, self, and person 151
- 9.5 The development of concrete reasonableness 155
- 9.6 God, science, and religion 157

Notes 165
Bibliography 171
Index 175

ABBREVIATIONS

CN volume: page. *Charles Sanders Peirce: Contributions to* The Nation. 4 Vols. Kenneth L. Ketner and James E. Cook, eds Lubbock, 1975–87.
CP volume: paragraph. *The Collected Papers of Charles Sanders Peirce.* 8 Vols. Vols. 1–6, ed. Charles Hartshorne and Paul Weiss. Vols. 7–8, ed. Arthur W. Burks. Cambridge, Mass., 1931–58.
EP volume: page. *The Essential Peirce: Selected Philosophical Writings.* 2 Vols. Vol. 1. ed. Nathan Houser and Christian Kloesel. Vol. 2, ed. Peirce Edition Project. Bloomington, 1992–98.
HPPLS volume: page. *Historical Perspectives on Peirce's Logic of Science.* 2 Vols. ed. Carolyn Eisele. The Hague, 1985.
NEM volume: page. *The New Elements of Mathematics*, 4 Vols. in 5. ed. Carolyn Eisele. The Hague, 1976.
PM *Philosophy of Mathematics: Selected Writings.* ed. Matthew Moore Bloomington, 2010.
R followed by Robin catalogue and sheet number. Manuscripts held in the Houghton Library of Harvard University, as identified by Richard Robin, *Annotated Catalogue of the Papers of Charles S. Peirce.* Amherst, 1967, and in Richard Robin, "The Peirce papers: a supplementary catalogue," *Transactions of the C. S. Peirce Society* 7 (1971): 37–57.
RLT *Reasoning and the Logic of Things: The Cambridge Conferences Lectures of 1898*, ed. Kenneth L. Ketner. Cambridge, Mass., 1992.
SS *Semiotic and Significs: The Correspondence between Charles S. Peirce and Victoria Lady Welby*, ed. Charles S. Hardwick. Bloomington, 1977.
W volume: page. *The Writings of Charles S. Peirce*, ed. The Peirce Edition Project, 7 Vols. to date. Bloomington, 1982–2010.

CHAPTER ONE

Life and work

In the early morning of 29 December 1914, a young graduate student from Harvard and a local farmer with a droopy moustache sped on a horse-drawn sled to the Port Jervis train station. They carried with them roughly a thousand books and two heavy crates of manuscripts that belonged to the American philosopher Charles Sanders Peirce (pronounced "purse") who had died that spring. The two crates of manuscripts would establish Peirce as one of the great Western philosophers. During his life, Peirce was highly regarded as a scientist and as a logician, but not too much was known of his philosophy, as most of it had remained unpublished.

Charles Peirce was born in Cambridge, Massachusetts, on 10 September 1839, as the second son of the renowned mathematician and astronomer Benjamin Peirce. Charles Peirce (hereafter referred to as 'Peirce' the focus of this book) was far from a bookish philosopher and the scope of his work is staggering. He did pioneering work on the magnitude of stars and the form of the Milky Way. He worked extensively determining the exact shape of the earth, designing instruments, and improving methodologies. He invented a new map projection that gave a world map with a minimum distortion of the distance between any two points. He was a pioneer in mathematical logic and mathematical economy, did important work on Shakespearean pronunciation, engaged in experimental psychology, wrote several books on logic and mathematics (none of which were published), gave lectures on the history of science, developed a bleaching process for wood pulp, wrote on spelling reform, made calculations for a suspension bridge over the Hudson river, and was the first to use a wavelength of light to determine the exact length of the meter. Almost as an aside, in a short letter to his former student Alan Marquand, Peirce invented the electronic switching-circuit computer—until then computing machines had been wholly mechanical (W5:421–23). However, none of these accomplishments really helped Peirce, who died in abject poverty and almost completely forgotten in a small town called Milford, Pennsylvania, on 19 April 1914. Peirce was survived only by his second wife (whose identity is still a mystery) and by a disarray of over a hundred thousand manuscript pages. The American philosopher Josiah Royce, who was deeply indebted to Peirce's thought, worked hard to raise money for Peirce's papers and library, and for the less than impressive sum of five hundred dollars the books and papers went to Harvard, first by sled and then by train. Though the process of getting Peirce's unpublished writings into print is slow and not without controversy, it is already undeniable that he is a philosopher of great magnitude whose writings are bound to significantly alter the philosophical landscape.

This book aims to guide the reader through Peirce's philosophy. There are various ways of doing this. One can discuss it chronologically, carefully tracing the important steps he takes during the six decades he is working on philosophical and other issues.[1] Such an approach has great advantages. It will show the external and internal strains that cause pivotal shifts in his position, which leads to a better understanding of what he does and why. But as Peirce is active in so many areas it is also a complicated story, and a story that depends heavily on a good understanding of the main currents of thought in his time. Peirce does not write in a vacuum. He is keenly aware of what is going on in mathematics and in the sciences, and he makes extensive use of it.

Alternatively, one can highlight certain issues, for instance those where Peirce is most innovative or most influential. The problem with such a "greatest hits" approach is that it fails to show the systematic character of his work. A third approach is to focus on its systematic character and discuss Peirce's contributions in the framework of it. This is the approach taken in this book. Peirce spends an inordinate amount of time classifying the sciences and positioning philosophy among them. Choosing Peirce's classification of the sciences, which includes an ordered classification of philosophical activities, and structuring the discussion of his work around it, has the further advantage that one can make rather detailed detours without losing sight of the whole.

1.1 The birth of a polymath

Peirce is one of a handful in the history of thought who can truly be called a universal intellect. Robert Crease calls him "a prolific and perpetually overextended polymath," and that pretty well sums him up.[2] He is deeply involved in the main currents of thought (mathematics, logic, experimental science), most of which are in rapid transition, and he makes significant contributions to a great variety of areas. Some have called Peirce the American Aristotle, others the American Leibniz,[3] and it would certainly be no less appropriate to call him the American Leonardo, after that most famous of polymaths Leonardo da Vinci.

Typically, the making of a polymath begins at childhood, and that's true here as well. Peirce's father was a Harvard mathematician and astronomer who played a key role in the establishment of a scientific community within the US.[4] He was involved in the creation of the National Academy of Sciences and the Smithsonian Institution, and from 1867 to 1874 he was in charge of the US Coast Survey, which at the time was America's premier scientific institution. Because of this, and because his father was a polymath of sorts as well, Peirce is already at a young age exposed to the workings of science. As he later reminisces: "all the leading men of science, particularly astronomers and physicists, resorted to our house; so that I was brought up in an atmosphere of science. But my father was a broad man and we were intimate with literary people too" (SS:113).

Benjamin Peirce saw early on that young Charles was gifted and he took an active role in his early education. Benjamin was an unconventional teacher who taught his students by inspiring them rather than by carefully guiding them through proofs and to the solutions of problems. He was known to throw his proofs and solutions rapidly onto the blackboard, preferring quick and elegant solutions, and speedily erasing what he had written the moment he ran out of space. The common opinion was that the rings on Peirce's ladder stood too far apart and that though he ascended easily most others fell through. Those who fell through, however, still spoke highly of him and were grateful to have been his student. About the education he receives from his father, Peirce later remarks: "He very seldom could be entrapped into disclosing to me any theorem or rule of arithmetic. He would give an example; but the rest I must think out for myself" (R619:5). To help him with the latter, Peirce continues, "[my father] took great pains to teach me concentration of mind and to keep my attention upon the strain for a long time. From time to time he would put me to the test by keeping me playing rapid games of double-dummy from ten in the evening until sunrise, and sharply criticizing every error" (id.). About the extent of his father's influence, Peirce later writes: "He educated me, and if I do anything it will be his work" (R1608:2).

Hence, from early on Peirce is put into the habit of thinking things out for himself. Though he is an avid reader with a solid knowledge of the history of science and philosophy, and kept up with contemporary work, he retains this habit of thinking things through in his own way, which contributes greatly to his originality as a thinker.

This habit of thinking things out for himself gets a major boost when at the age of twelve his uncle Charles Henry Peirce helped him set up a chemistry laboratory at home. Charles Henry had been a student and assistant of Eben Horsford who had introduced Justus von Liebig's experimental method of teaching at Harvard (Horsford had studied with Liebig in Germany). Rejecting the purely theoretical way chemistry was being taught, Liebig gave each student a series of bottles marked with the letters of the alphabet. The student was asked to analyze the contents of each bottle, using as the sole guide an introductory textbook in qualitative analysis. Over the years, the number of bottles in Liebig's course had grown to a hundred and it took the average student about a year to complete the exercise. It was on this model that Peirce's home laboratory was set up, together with a copy of his uncle's translation of Stöckhardt's *Principles of Chemistry*.

Though Liebig's method of teaching was strictly an exercise in chemical analysis, it could be applied to experimental science more broadly. Eben Horsford picked up on this. He used the method not only in his own teaching, but when he founded the Lawrence Scientific School at Harvard—a school Peirce graduates from in 1863—he modeled the entire school after Liebig's method. In 1869, the impact of Liebig's method widened even further when

Charles Eliot—also a student of Horsford and Peirce's chemistry teacher at Lawrence Scientific—becomes President of Harvard. Eliot remains president for 40 years, making Harvard the first American university to be solidly grounded in the principles of experimental science. Briefly, already at the age of twelve, while experimenting with Liebig's bottles, Peirce is deeply immersing himself in the experimental method. This happens at a time when that method itself and the science it generates are also still in their infancy. Thus, a brilliant mind that still possesses the openness of youth finds before him a fertile land that lies mostly untilled. Moreover, the Liebig method is a very practical way of learning chemical analysis, one where the difference in the contents of the bottles is determined by the practical consequences of the various operations performed upon them. As we will see in the chapters that follow, this too leaves its mark on how Peirce comes to see not only science but also philosophy.

Also at the age of twelve, Peirce reads Richard Whately's *Elements of Logic,* a work that revitalized the study of logic in the English-speaking world.[5] Peirce finds the book in his older brother's room and promptly devours it. Later he repeatedly says that from then on logic was his strongest passion. For instance, when working as a scientist, Peirce retains a strong focus on methodology, making it his first priority to penetrate into the logic of things. As with chemistry, Peirce's introduction to logic also comes when the discipline is in the process of a dramatic transformation. It is around this time that the British mathematician George Boole develops an algebra for logic, giving logic a mathematical grounding that not only frees it from the restraints of Aristotelian syllogisms but that also opens the door for extensive new research. Peirce, who thanks to his father already had an affinity for mathematics, comes to play an important role in this. Although Whately's logic is predominantly Aristotelian, one can also discern a strong influence of John Locke. Whately rejected, for instance, the problematic notion of "abstract ideas," arguing instead that we think in signs.[6] Hence, we can find in Whately some of the early seeds of Peirce's semeiotics (Chapter 5).

Benjamin Peirce did not share his son's fascination for logic. In fact he had a very low opinion of logic, preferring instead "to draw directly upon the geometrical instinct" (echoes of this return in Peirce's logical graphs; Section 4.7).[7] Benjamin Peirce also had a low opinion of the reasoning of philosophers more generally, and time and time again he would force his son to "recognize the extremely loose reasoning common to the philosophers" (CP2.9). After Whately's logic, Peirce's first readings in philosophy are Friedrich Schiller's *Aesthetic Letters* and Immanuel Kant's *Critique of Pure Reason*. It was Schiller who introduces Peirce to Kant, and he begins reading Kant's first *Critique* shortly before his seventeenth birthday. Peirce spends roughly three years studying the first *Critique*, a process during which his father proves very influential. As Peirce puts it: "[the *Critique of Pure Reason*] was sort of a Bible to me; and if my father had not exposed the weaknesses of some of its arguments, I do not know to what lengths my worship of it might not have gone" (R619:10f). Notwithstanding the sobering influence of his father, Kant continues to have a far-reaching and profound influence on Peirce's thought.

Peirce goes to Harvard at sixteen. At Harvard the habit his father instilled in him—that of seeking his own way intellectually—works against him, and he performs rather poorly. In 1858, he joins a local expedition of the Coast Survey, which is not uncommon at the time for scientifically inclined students. It is there that Peirce finds his stride; it proves the beginning of a 30-year career as a scientist. In July 1861, Peirce received his first official appointment as a lowly paid computer, but he quickly moves up. In a little over a decade he is in charge of gravitational research and is promoted to the Survey's highest rank, that of Assistant to the Superintendant. Also in 1861, Peirce enters Harvard's Lawrence Scientific School to study chemistry. Two years later he graduates summa cum laude.

1.2 An outsider

Being found a genius also has its darker side. From early on Peirce is constantly told he is a genius and he is treated as such, and this significantly affects how he comes to see himself. Especially during the first half of his life it leaves a strong mark on his relationships with others, though other personality traits also contribute to this. Although Peirce considers himself a genius, and spends much time studying what he called "great men," he typically explains his own success as a thinker in terms of his great power of concentration and a dogged, pedestrian persistence which he jokingly calls Peirce-istance, or Peirce-everance.

George Whalley, the editor of the works of Coleridge, once remarked that what sets the genius apart is "not the sheer quantity of learning . . . but the incandescence, the opulence, the extravagant gratuitousness, the rapidity of mind."[8] Peirce's close friend William James makes a similar observation about Peirce when he characterizes Peirce's 1903 Lowell lectures as "flashes of brilliant light relieved against Cimmerian darkness."[9] Ralph Waldo Emerson, one of the literary figures that frequented the young Peirce's home, points out another aspect of genius that aptly applies to Peirce: "Genius is always sufficiently the enemy of genius by over-influence."[10] Although Ian Hacking overstates his case when he describes Peirce as a wild man who began almost everything and finished almost nothing,[11] Emerson's observation is much of the reason why the systematic philosopher never completed a book about his philosophy—he is constantly moving in new directions, never satisfied with what he had written.

Overall Peirce provides a painful example of a great thinker with a failed career. Apart from a brief stint as a lecturer in logic at Johns Hopkins (1879–84), he never holds a university position. An initially brilliant career at the Coast Survey comes to a sudden and graceless end in 1891, after roughly 30 years of service. Peirce works the last third of his life as an independent scholar, which forces him to constantly struggle for money. During this period, he writes mostly for a living, gives lectures, and does occasional freelance work in a variety of fields. In 1887, while he is still working for the Coast Survey, he moves to Milford, Pennsylvania, a small resort town not far from the Port Jervis train station, from which it is only a few hours to New York City. Just outside Milford, he purchases a small farmhouse with quite a bit of land. The house becomes an obsession, and at the time of his death it had grown into a 25-room mansion.

The story of Peirce's life is complicated and one that still needs to be told.[12] There are many theories on why he fell from grace. He had a difficult personality. He had powerful enemies, including Harvard President Charles Eliot and Simon Newcomb (the latter became America's premier scientist). He was considered a deeply immoral man and a bad role model for students when he married his mistress, a mysterious French woman with whom he had been living openly, only two days after he divorced his first wife (even though she left him seven years before). Irrespective of his personality traits, his enemies, and the moral reprobation, the mere fact that during the last third of his life he lives in relative isolation and is not connected to a university is by itself enough to make him an outsider. Fortunately, he also has a few good friends. The latter include Harvard philosopher Josiah Royce, who is deeply influenced by Peirce and arranges for his library and papers to come to Harvard.

1.3 The Peirce papers

Peirce thought with his pen, he thought often, and he seldom threw anything away. The result is that upon his death he left behind an enormous mass of manuscripts. Estimates vary, but it is typically conjectured that there are over a hundred thousand manuscript pages preserved in Harvard's Houghton Library, with substantial deposits elsewhere. The history of the manuscripts may even be more complicated and controversial than Peirce's life.[13] From the start, the aim was to organize the manuscripts and extract from them material suitable for publication. This task proved overwhelming, not just because of the sheer volume of the papers, but also because of their disorganized state, Peirce's propensity to digress and leave things unfinished, and his constant reworking of issues. Martin Heidegger once described his own thoughts as *Holtzwege*, after the countless trails found in well-traveled woods, often so faint it is unclear whether they even are trails, and many leading nowhere.[14] More recently, Vincent Colapietro described Peirce's writing as a one-man jam session—it is restlessly experimental, improvisational, and prone to digression.[15] Both are apt descriptions, and it makes the task of any editor no easy one. Often there are endless variations on a theme, and frequently there is no clear winner as different strands have different things to offer. Peirce once described himself as having the persistence of a wasp in a bottle, and this shows in his writings.

Initially, Josiah Royce took charge of the manuscripts, but about a year into the project he suddenly passed away himself. Royce's graduate student W. Fergus Kernan did much of the initial sorting, but soon left to fight in World War I. After that the manuscripts fell into disarray. At the end of the 1920s, when Charles Hartshorne and Paul Weiss began working on what was to become their six-volume *Collected Papers,* they found that someone had gathered everything in a few large piles. The sheer quantity of the material and their disorganized state made it impossible to extract from them six volumes that would do justice to Peirce's thought. Because so few manuscripts were dated, the two editors decided on a thematic approach, following Peirce's classification of the sciences. And because they had so little space, they typically limited themselves to what they thought was the best text on a certain subject. This meant that often only parts of documents were included. The edition brings a large portion of Peirce's philosophical work together (published as well as unpublished), but it does so in a manner that gives the impression of an undisciplined thinker who was prone to contradict himself without noticing it. This greatly affected the reception of Peirce's work. Another negative consequence is that with the *Collected Papers* published, the manuscripts were thought to be of no more scholarly value and quite a number of them were given away as mementos.

In the late 1950s, Arthur Burks edited two more volumes and Max Fisch was enlisted to write an intellectual biography that was to form the capstone to the edition. Fisch quickly discovered that a systematic study of Peirce based on the *Collected Papers* was impossible, and a new effort ensued to organize the manuscripts. In 1967, this resulted in Richard Robin's *Annotated Catalogue of the Papers of Charles S. Peirce,* which also relied for its organizing principle on Peirce's classification of the sciences. The catalogue became the basis of a microfilm edition, so that by the end of the 1960s the bulk of the material held at Harvard was more widely accessible. The next large-scale editions of Peirce's works are Carolyn Eisele's *New Elements of Mathematics* (5 vols in 4) and the four-volume *Contributions to The Nation*, edited by Kenneth Ketner and James Cook. Both editions appeared in the 1970s. The first contains Peirce's extensive work in mathematics; the second contains the many book reviews he wrote for *The Nation*. Fisch, however, realized that to understand Peirce's philosophy we must be able to follow the trajectory of his thought. This resulted in a project on a much grander scale: *The Writings of Charles S. Peirce: A Chronological Edition*. This edition, which is projected to span 30 volumes, depends heavily on a far-reaching reorganization of the manuscripts in which the papers held at Harvard and elsewhere are ordered chronologically. This edition, which is still a selective edition (publishing everything would require at least a hundred volumes), is not limited to Peirce's philosophical writings—as if they can neatly be separated from the rest—but covers also the work he did in the sciences, in mathematics, and in other areas.

1.4 Classifying the sciences

In good nineteenth-century fashion, Peirce spends much time and effort devising a classification of the sciences. However, before discussing his classification we should see what he means by classification and by science. Peirce does not aim for some abstract classification in which any conceivable science has its preordained pigeonhole, but he aims more modestly for a concrete classification of the sciences insofar as they are "the actual living occupation of an actual living group of men" (R1334:13). Put differently, his classification is an empirical one that is based on what is taking place in terms of living scientific activity, and in this sense it is very similar to botanical and zoological classifications. Such natural classifications can be contrasted with artificial classifications where the criteria for inclusion are determined beforehand.

So what types of scientific activity are taking place? For our purpose here it suffices to say that when Peirce speaks of a science he means "life devoted to the pursuit of truth according to the best known methods on the part of a group of men who understand one another's ideas and works as no outsider can" (R1334:14). With the latter he means that their studies are so closely allied "that any one could take up the problem of any other after some months of special preparation" (R1334:15), and that they understand each other's work to the point of being thoroughly conversant about it with one another. It is further important to note that Peirce's interpretation of science is a very broad one. It includes any endeavor where one is devoted to the pursuit of truth, whether this is the homicide detective searching for a killer, the historian looking for the identity of Jack the Ripper, the geneticist seeking to uncover the sequence of DNA, or the astrophysicist who wants to understand the nature of black holes. Often what unites a group of scientists is a familiarity with certain theories, a shared language, or a skill in the use of certain instruments or in making particular sorts of observations; in brief, it's a division according to methods, ideas, and instruments (CD:5379). What distinguishes, say, the specialist in optics from the astronomer, is that the former is intimately familiar with the principles on which the latter's instruments are based. The astronomer lacks the conversancy in optical theory that the specialist in optics has, while the specialist in optics lacks the astronomer's skill of using telescopes to extract knowledge from the heavens. As this classification is based on scientific practices and the communicability of ideas, its boundaries will be vague and open to revision when practices change or when future inquiry leads to new areas of cooperation. Moreover, as with the evolution of biological species, the classes are not defined in terms of some ideal, suggesting that it is our task to bring us closer to that ideal.

Peirce's classification of the sciences is thus one according to actual scientific *practices,* and not one according to the *objects* of scientific knowledge, whether they are actual or merely possible. Peirce thereby rejects the standard account on which science is defined as systematized knowledge. Moreover, as we shall see in Chapter 6, he further rejects the idea that science can be defined in terms of a specific method, the so-called scientific method.

So how does Peirce classify the sciences? His first division is between the sciences of discovery (or the heuretic sciences), the sciences of review, and the practical sciences. For Peirce, *the sciences of discovery* exemplify science in its purest sense. Their aim is the acquisition of positive knowledge solely for the sake of gaining knowledge. *The sciences of review* seek to draw together the fragmented discoveries made in the heuretic sciences and make them available to a wider audience. It is here also that we find broader reflections upon and critical assessments of the work done in the narrowly focused heuretic sciences. Peirce's classification of the sciences belongs to the sciences of review, as do similar enterprises of August Comte and Herbert Spencer. *The practical sciences,* finally, seek to meet some human need. A good example is civil engineering, which uses the findings of the heuristic science of analytical mechanics for some practical application, like the construction of a skyscraper or suspension bridge. This third area is by far the largest and most people who call themselves scientists fall in it.

Peirce's interest is in the heuretic sciences and it is important to keep this in mind, otherwise one might mistakenly conclude that, for Peirce, all attempts to apply knowledge are suspect and that we should only search for disinterested knowledge. What Peirce *is* objecting to is to let practical considerations of purpose affect how knowledge is acquired in the *heuretic* sciences. I return to this in Chapter 6.

The first division in the heuretic sciences, or the sciences of discovery, is between mathematics and what Peirce calls, following Comte, the positive sciences. The positive sciences seek to affirm or deny, in a categorical proposition, something of some subject, such as, "cows have four stomachs," "the mutual forces of action and reaction between two bodies are equal but opposite and collinear," "Mount Everest is the tallest mountain on Earth," and "beriberi is not caused by an infectious agent." In Peirce's view, mathematics has a very different aim. In mathematics, we make no positive assertions of fact. It is purely the study of hypothetical or conditional propositions. The mathematician, Peirce explains, "makes no external observations, nor asserts anything as a real fact. When the mathematician deals with facts, they become for him mere 'hypotheses'; for with their truth he refuses to concern himself" (CP3.428). By making this move, Peirce rejects the view of Comte and positivists and empiricists more generally, who consider mathematics the most general and most fundamental of the positive sciences. Peirce's conception of mathematics, as well as its relation to the positive sciences, is discussed in Chapter 2.

Peirce next divides the positive sciences into philosophy and the special sciences. The special sciences are those that require special equipment or familiarity with certain theories, terminology, or methods. Typical examples are particle physics, microbiology, and linguistics. Peirce divides the special sciences in two parallel classes: the physical sciences and the psychical sciences. Philosophy, in contrast, requires no specialized equipment or background knowledge. It is nothing but "a more attentive scrutiny and comparison of the facts of everyday life" (EP2:146). In principle anyone can do it. Philosophy is subdivided in phenomenology, the normative sciences (esthetics, ethics, and logic), and metaphysics. The aim of the first is "to draw up an inventory of appearances without going into any investigation of their truth" (CP2.120); that of the second to study how these phenomena relate to certain ends (traditionally these are beauty, goodness, and truth); that of the third to develop a *Weltanschauung* that can form the basis for the special sciences. According to Peirce, we cannot avoid having a metaphysics; we can only fail to make it explicit. Note that the kind of metaphysics Peirce has in mind here is a *scientific* metaphysics. Peirce's metaphysics is discussed in Chapters 8 and 9.

The above division gives the following sequence of the sciences of discovery. First we have a division between mathematics and the positive sciences. The latter are further divided into phenomenology, esthetics, ethics, logic, and metaphysics, after which comes the special sciences parallel divided into the physical and the psychical sciences. Each of the positive sciences depends on those that precede it for its grounding principles while providing the latter with fresh material to contemplate. The relation is thus not one-directional. For instance, though logic is a more basic science than mechanics, Peirce observes that from Plato and Aristotle onward logic made no significant progress until around 1590, when Galileo developed the science of dynamics. And he further adds that, "it was the study of dynamics, more than anything else, which gradually taught men to reason better on all subjects" (R447:5). Moreover all the positive sciences can use mathematics.

Before continuing, a few words should be said on Peirce's ethics of terminology. Peirce is often berated for his penchant for complicated neologisms, and not infrequently he coins words to never use them again. This is true, for instance with *heurospude, taxospude,* and *prattospude,* which denote respectively the sciences of discovery, the sciences of review, and the practical sciences (R1334:25). But those who berate him do not give him enough credit. Peirce observes that biology and chemistry made their significant advances only after they developed a clear nomenclature, and he is keenly aware that many philosophical problems are caused, or their solutions hampered, by poor terminology and a continual and often implicit redefining of terms. Peirce, who is himself trained as a chemist, envisions for philosophy a terminology similar to chemistry, with an almost modular construction and a system of prefixes and suffixes. He also maintains that once a term is introduced one should stay as close as possible to the meaning that was then given to it.

CHAPTER TWO

Mathematics and philosophy

In the opening chapter, we saw that when classifying the sciences of discovery Peirce sets mathematics apart from the other sciences, which he calls the positive sciences. The aim of the positive sciences is to increase our knowledge of the actual universe. Mathematics, as Peirce envisions it, is not confined in this way. Its aim is not to study how things are, have been, or will be but to study purely hypothetical states of things, and for that it does not matter how far they stray from the world we experience. As noted, by separating mathematics from the positive sciences, Peirce departs from Comte and others who consider mathematics the most abstract and the most basic of the positive sciences.

In part what causes Peirce's break with Comte is the transformation of mathematics that takes place in the nineteenth century. The old view of mathematics as the science that describes nature in its most general terms—that is, only insofar as things can be counted or measured—is no longer tenable. For instance, non-Euclidean geometries that allow us to work with spaces very different from the physical space we are accustomed to, and consistent algebras that include things like the square root of minus one, cause mathematics to depart radically from the world of sense and consequently also from our intuitions (for Peirce our intuitions are products of biological evolution). The result is that at the close of the nineteenth century mathematics is a very different discipline than what it was at the beginning of that century.

Peirce is well versed in mathematics. As we saw in Chapter 1, his father used his mathematical skills to persistently attack the poor reasoning of the philosophers to whom the young Peirce took a liking. This made a deep impression and during the course of his life Peirce continues to play close attention to mathematics, so much so that in the 1880s James Joseph Sylvester, the great mathematician of the day, called him "a far greater mathematician than his father."[1] Although during his life little of Peirce's work in mathematics is published, a wealth of material survives among his unpublished papers, including two completed book manuscripts.[2] A project Peirce is long engaged in is to publish a textbook, *The New Elements,* that incorporates the recent transformation of mathematics, and that is to replace Euclid's *Elements,* which after two millennia is still the standard mathematics textbook.

In the current chapter, we look at Peirce's views on mathematics, as some understanding of Peirce's views on mathematics is crucial for an adequate understanding of his philosophy. Philosophers often look at mathematics as the model of good reasoning. This is very evident in Spinoza's *Ethics*, which even mimics Euclid's *Elements* in its structure of definitions, axioms, and theorems. Peirce agrees that mathematical reasoning is crucial for philosophy—and his classification of the sciences shows as much—but he also observes that philosophers often have no adequate understanding of what mathematical reasoning consists in, and that most are oblivious of the recent changes that had taken place in mathematics and their philosophic repercussions.

Philosophy, Peirce writes, "requires exact thought, and all exact thought is mathematical thought" (R438:3). Consequently, Peirce seeks to introduce mathematical exactitude into philosophy in part as a means of reducing error:

> All danger of error in philosophy will be reduced to a minimum by treating the problems as mathematically as possible, that is, by constructing some sort of a diagram representing that which is supposed to be open to the observation of every scientific intelligence, and thereupon mathematically,—that is, intuitionally,—deducing the consequences of that hypothesis. (R787:7)

The latter part of this quotation gives some insight in what Peirce takes mathematical reasoning to be. It involves the construction and observation of and experimentation upon diagrams. This notion that mathematical reasoning is diagrammatic reasoning goes back to Peirce's reading of Kant, ironically one of the loose thinkers his father warned him against (Section 1.1).

2.1 Kant's conception of mathematics

Kant writes his *Critique of Pure Reason* as a safeguard against bad philosophical reasoning. Regarding straightforward empirical matters, Kant observes, no such critique is needed as experience quickly puts our theories to the test. Mathematics does not need such a critique either, because mathematical reasoning is "exhibited *in concreto* in pure intuition, so that everything unfounded and arbitrary in [it] is at once exposed."[3] In philosophy, however, where our conclusions are not constantly checked by experience and our reasoning is not guided by our a priori intuition, a critique of reasoning (and of the elements used in reasoning) is direly needed. To address this Kant writes the *Critique of Pure Reason*. Kant moreover believes, in direct contrast to Peirce, that the use of mathematical reasoning to address philosophical issues is a prime source of error in philosophy, and he goes to great lengths to explain why mathematical reasoning cannot be used to that purpose. In this section, I briefly discuss Kant's division between philosophical and mathematical reasoning, and highlight some points where Peirce departs from Kant.

Kant sees philosophical reasoning as a strictly discursive enterprise. We form concepts based on our empirical intuition and our interaction with the world. However, all we can do with these concepts is to sort under them what appears to us within experience, or what we envision when applying our empirical intuition—a process that typically causes us to sharpen or revise the concepts we start off with. Thus, our concept of gold allows us to distinguish what is gold from what is not, and our experience in drawing that distinction allows us to sharpen or refine our concept of gold. For Kant, the only way we can go beyond our concept of gold (as a dense shiny yellow metal) is through a reflection on the appearances we encounter and on the concepts we have connected with it (in this case dense, shiny, yellow, and metal). Thus, when we discover that its yellow color is due to impurities, that gold dissolves in *aqua regia*, or that its atomic number is 79, we change our concept of gold accordingly. This type of reasoning is a posteriori in that it depends on empirical data, and as such it can only generate synthetic knowledge that is contingent. It cannot lead to necessary knowledge. For Kant, who like Peirce considers philosophy a positive science, philosophical concepts are of this kind. However, since they are typically abstracted syntheses of empirical intuitions, judgments that contain them cannot easily be undermined by empirical observation.

Mathematical reasoning is very different from this. Whereas in philosophy we reason from concepts, in mathematics we reason, as Kant puts it, *from the construction of concepts within pure intuition*. The following example of Kant shows what he means by this.[4] Let us begin with the discursive concept of a triangle as a closed chain of three straight, finite line segments on a single plane, and ask how the sum of the three interior angles formed by these three line segments relates to a right angle. To answer this question we begin by drawing, or constructing, a figure of the triangle in accordance with what Kant calls our pure intuition (see Figure 2.1a). Early on, in the Transcendental Aesthetic, Kant argues that we have an a priori, or pure, intuition of space, one that does not depend on any empirical knowledge or any empirical intuitions. We also have an a priori intuition of time.

We continue our proof by extending one of the line segments on both sides, and add an entirely new line parallel to this extended line, intersecting the point where the other two line segments meet (Figure 2.1b). Now we can see immediately that the sum of angles B

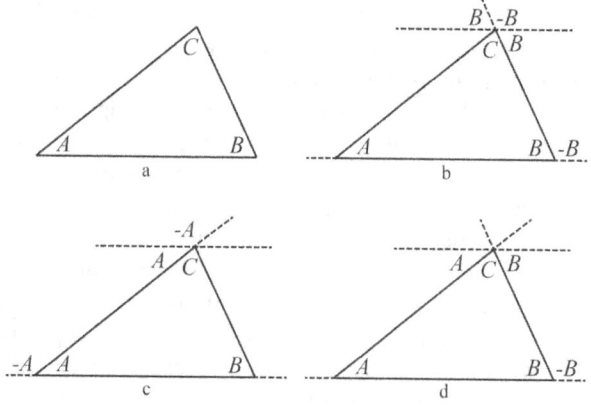

FIGURE 2.1 *Triangles.*

and 2B, on line segment AB equals the sum of two right angles (right angles are formed when a line intersects another perpendicularly). Next extending line BC beyond C, we can see immediately that this repeats itself where BC intersects the line that runs through C. Next we observe that because BC is a straight line too, the angle right adjacent to C must again be equal to B. We can then go through the exact same routine for angle A by extending AC and showing that the angle left adjacent to C is equal to A (Figure 2.1c). This completes our proof that the sum of the angles A, B, and C is equivalent to the sum of two right angles (Figure 2.1d).

A few observations can be made. First, as is clear from the example, the construction goes well beyond what is explicitly expressed in the concept we started off with. Second, the argument does not proceed syllogistically, that is, by substituting concepts for concepts, as in: "All men are mortal"; "Socrates is a man," hence "Socrates is mortal." Instead, to use Kant's terminology, we *construct* a concept; that is, we exhibit a priori the intuition that corresponds to the concept, which is something we can do because of our already existing intuition of space and time. In the process, we create a *single* object that is representative of all possible pure intuitions relating to that concept. This allows Kant to maintain that the conclusions that are being drawn are necessary and not merely contingent as with empirical arguments. Third, this construction is essential to the argument. It is not merely an auxiliary tool to facilitate our mathematical reasoning, but it forms the very core of that reasoning. In fact, Kant denies that we can reach conclusions like the one above through a chain of syllogisms. Fourth, Kant's use of pure intuition allows him to ignore those elements of the created objects that are of an empirical nature, such as the color or the thickness of the lines, or the lines drawn not being perfectly straight, up to the point that the conclusion may be visibly false for the actual figure drawn (which typically happens when we make a quick sketch on a napkin). Fifth, mathematical reasoning, though a priori, allows us to gain new insights that carry us beyond the concepts we began with. In Kant's terminology, mathematics is thus both a priori and synthetic. This means that, for Kant, mathematics is a science of discovery.

Though geometry best exhibits this type of reasoning, Kant extends it to other areas of mathematics as well. But that is also where it ends. Most importantly, Kant believes that mathematical reasoning is not applicable within philosophy, including logic. In philosophy, we should limit ourselves to the type of discursive reasoning described above. Mathematics realizes its concepts within pure intuition, but this also means that its application is limited to pure intuition. Philosophy can do neither. It cannot realize its concepts within pure intuition, as it depends for its insights on what is given to us through the senses, and it cannot limit the application of its concepts to the realm of pure intuition without giving up on its mission of gaining knowledge of the empirical world. For Kant, the divide is radical. In fact, the difference between the two types of reasoning is so great, and what they try to establish so different, that at least in mathematics and philosophy they cannot be combined.[5] Whereas the propensity of philosophers to use mathematical reasoning only leads to extravagance and error, applying the discursive method of philosophy to mathematical problems avoids error, but only because it is perfectly vacuous. The application of discursive reasoning in mathematics can never go beyond a purely analytic explication of concepts, and thus can never yield any new knowledge.

Though Peirce finds much in Kant that he likes, he disagrees with Kant at crucial junctions, concluding not just that mathematical reasoning can be used in philosophy, but that it is even indispensible for it—one cannot do philosophy without engaging in mathematical reasoning. Hence, it is with a chapter on Peirce's conception of mathematics that we begin.

2.2 The exact study of ideal states of things

As noted, mathematics was long considered the science that gives us the most abstract description of the world, as it only studied things insofar as we can measure or count them. Because of this, mathematics was traditionally defined as the science of quantity—continuous quantities in the case of geometry and discrete quantities in the case of arithmetic. The developments in the nineteenth century made this view of mathematics as the metrics of nature no longer tenable. This had a liberating effect. It freed mathematicians from the requirement that their products must reflect the natural world. This liberation caused Georg Cantor, with whose work Peirce is very familiar, to proclaim that freedom is the essence of mathematics:

"Mathematics is perfectly free in its development and is subject only to the obvious consideration that its concepts must be free from contradictions in themselves, as well as definitely and orderly related by means of definitions to the previously existing and established concepts."[6] The natural world no longer constrained mathematics.

In his *Linear Associative Algebra,* Peirce's father defined mathematics as "the science which draws necessary conclusions."[7] This definition forms the basis of Peirce's own conception of mathematics. According to Peirce, his father's definition makes mathematics the study of purely hypothetical states of things: "Since it is impossible to draw necessary conclusions except from perfect knowledge, and no knowledge of the real world can be perfect, it follows that, according to this definition mathematics must exclusively relate to the substance of hypotheses" (PM:7). For Peirce, these hypotheses are mere mental creations, and he even goes as far as to state that except for their precision, clearness, and consistency, they are not unlike dreams (R17:7).

Benjamin Peirce concluded from his definition that neither the discovery of laws nor the framing of theories properly belongs to mathematics.[8] At this point Peirce departs from his father, maintaining that mathematics includes *both* the framing of theories *and* the deduction of their consequences. In accordance with his natural classification of the sciences (Section 1.4), Peirce argues that we should look at mathematics as the living enterprise mathematicians are actually engaged in. If we look at mathematics this way, Peirce continues, we naturally include "everything that is an indispensible part of the mathematician's business; and therefore we must include the *formulation* of his hypotheses as well as the tracing out of their consequences" (PM:91). This means that, for Charles Peirce, mathematics deals with far more than drawing necessary conclusions.

The best way to examine Peirce's broader conception of mathematics is to see how it connects with the positive sciences, as it is there that mathematicians find their raw material. In Peirce's view, pure mathematics is ultimately a product of applied mathematics. This is how Peirce sketches the typical trajectory: "the business of the mathematician lies with exact ideas, or hypotheses, which he first frames upon the suggestion of some practical problem, then traces out their consequences, and ultimately generalizes" (R188:2). On this view, when physicists, meteorologists, or economists are faced with a complicated problem they call the mathematician for help.

The mathematician then seeks to construct a state of things that is far simpler than the complex reality that is being investigated, while ensuring that this simplification does not affect the practical answer that is being sought. In this way mathematicians provide scientists with a skeleton models—or hypotheses, as Peirce calls them—that can be studied instead of the phenomena themselves in all their fortuitous detail. Since the hypothesis we want the mathematician to consider should be one that is well suited for mathematical treatment, Peirce argues that framing the hypothesis should fall under the purview of mathematics rather than the empirical science the hypothesis is meant to serve. As Peirce puts it:

> The results of experience have to be simplified, generalized, and severed from fact so as to be perfect ideas before they are suited to mathematical use. They have, in short, to be adapted to the powers of mathematics and of the mathematician. It is only the mathematician who knows what these powers are; and consequently the framing of the mathematical hypotheses must be performed by the mathematician. (R17:6f)

Put briefly, framing such hypotheses does not require more detailed empirical work, but calls for mathematical imagination; that is, "the power of distinctly picturing to ourselves intricate configurations" (R252:20).

As for the nature of the hypothesis arrived at, Peirce observes the following:

> The hypothesis . . . must have such a degree of definiteness as to permit formal deductions. . . . In other respects, the less definite the hypothesis is, the better. Thus, it would be a hindrance rather than a help to suppose a geometrical figure to have any particular color. Finally, the hypothesis of the mathematician is always of an intricate kind, so that all the relations involved cannot be seen at a glance. (NEM3:749)

Once the hypothesis is framed, the mathematician may generalize it to such a degree that it loses all connection with the practical problem that occasioned it. The development of non-Euclidean geometries and the use of imaginary numbers in arithmetic are clear examples of this.

Now what constitutes the powers of a mathematician? Peirce distinguishes three of them: imagination, concentration, and generalization. From these he extracts what he calls the duty of the mathematician, which is threefold:

1st, acting upon some suggestion, generally a practical one, he has to frame a supposition of an ideal state of things;
2nd, he has to study that ideal state of things, and find out what would be true in such a case;
3rd, he has to generalize upon that ideal state of things, and consider other ideal states of things differing in definite respects from the first. (NEM2:10)

In particular the power of generalization, which Peirce thinks "chiefly constitutes a mathematician" (R278a:91), is a skill difficult to attain. Peirce's emphasis on imagination, concentration, and generalization draws the attention away from the popular belief that it is the business of mathematicians to provide proofs.

Having explained how mathematical models come to be and having provided some insight into the mathematical mind-set, we can now characterize mathematics, as does Peirce, as "the exact study of ideal states of things" (NEM2:10).[9] That is to say, the practical motives that spurred the inquiry have been removed and all energy is directed to a study of the models themselves, irrespective of any relation they might have to anything external to them, and irrespective of any motives the inquirer might have other than studying the models entirely for their own sake.

For Peirce, the business of the mathematician thus consists of three parts: framing ideal states of things that are inspired by practical problems, determining what is true for these ideal states of things, and finally, studying them wholly in their own right without any reference or concern for what spurred their construction. In the next section, we examine what Peirce means by mathematical reasoning.

2.3 Mathematical reasoning

Like Kant, Peirce maintains that mathematical reasoning is diagrammatic. Having framed his hypothesis in general terms, the mathematician constructs a diagram, which Peirce takes to be "any visual skeleton form in which the relations of parts are perspicuously exhibited, and are distinguished by lettering or otherwise, and which has some signification, or at least some significance" (NEM2:345). Such a diagram, "will either be geometrical, that is, such that familiar spatial relations stand for the relations asserted in the premisses, or it will be algebraical, where the relations are expressed by objects which are imagined to be subject to certain rules, whether conventional or experiential" (CP2.778). On this view "a system of equations written under one another so that their relations may be seen at a glance" also constitutes a diagram (NEM2:345).

If mathematics is the study of diagrams, observation becomes a key ingredient of mathematical reasoning. This makes mathematics a true science of discovery, as relations may be observed that were not specified in the precept of construction. For instance, that any natural number can be represented as the sum of four squares is not something we deliberately put into the construction of these numbers, but is a relation that was discovered long after they had been in use.

Making observation a key ingredient of mathematical reasoning also opens the door for experimentation: performing acts on the diagram and observing the results. Such experimentation, Peirce argues, is akin to induction, with the difference that "it does not deal with a course of experience, but with whether or not a certain state of things can be imagined" (CP2.778). Experimentation introduces moreover an element of choice—something Peirce believes is true for all necessary reasoning (CP6.595). In sum, mathematical reasoning is experimental rather than reflective, and active rather than contemplative. Within mathematics we gain knowledge, Peirce argues, "not by a simple mental stare, or strain of mental vision," but by "manipulating on paper, or in the fancy, formulae or other diagrams" (CP4.86). Such experience alone, Peirce argues, brings out "the reason hidden within us," and as such " this experience only differs from what usually carries that name in that it brings out the reason hidden within and not the reason of Nature, as do the chemist's or physicist's experiments" (id.; also Section 9.5). Put differently, when experimenting on man-made diagrams, we just as much hit upon hard facts as when conducting experiments in nature. Using space as an example:

When the mathematician comes to study out this idea of space, he finds it does not follow his whims. He is compelled by some occult power within or behind the mind to recognize in it certain characters. All mathematicians, however antagonistic the ideas with which they set out, however unrelated the course of thought they pursue, come at last to the same conclusion. Space, though only an idea, seems to insist upon being thought in a certain way. It has its properties whether we like them or not. (R256:12)

The view that observation and experiment are crucial to mathematics is central to the mathematicians Peirce is close to while he is teaching at Johns Hopkins, and during the next two decades he spends much time and effort developing the philosophical underpinnings for this view. It also forms the basis for his more general contention that all valid necessary reasoning proceeds by experimentation upon diagrams and observing the results (CP1.54).

Consistent with the above, Peirce defines deduction as "an argument representing facts in the Premiss, such that when we come to represent them in a Diagram *we find ourselves compelled to represent the fact stated in the Conclusion*" (CP1.66; emphasis added). Or as he puts it elsewhere, deduction "consists in constructing an image or diagram in accordance with a general precept, in observing in that image certain relations of parts not explicitly laid down in the precept, and in convincing oneself that the same relations will always occur when that precept is followed out" (CP8.209). It is that what makes it *necessary* reasoning. The traditional syllogism is an example of this kind. It combines its elements in a structure that allows us to see their interconnection at a glance:

All humans are mortal;
Socrates is human;
Hence, Socrates is mortal.

We are compelled to accept the conclusion because we immediately *see* the connection between both premises and the conclusion, and we *see* that this connection hinges on the concept "human"

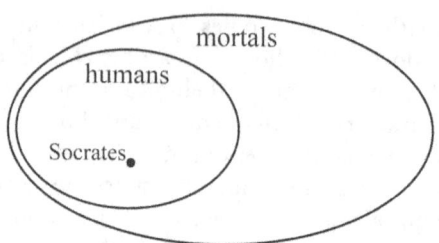

FIGURE 2.2 *Venn Diagram.*

being present in both premises. Instead of the above syllogism we could draw a Venn diagram. Here again we immediately *see* that given what we accept we cannot avoid concluding that Socrates is mortal.

In accordance with his discussion of mathematical reasoning, Peirce distinguishes two types of deduction, corollarial and theorematic, and he considers the discovery of this distinction his "first real discovery about mathematical procedure" (NEM4:49). A corollarial deduction "represents the conditions of the conclusion in a diagram and finds from the observation of this diagram, as it is, the truth of the conclusion" (CP2.267). The syllogism about Socrates is a good example. No one who sees it can reasonably doubt the conclusion. Theorematic deduction, in contrast, "is one which, having represented the conditions of the conclusion in a diagram, performs an ingenious experiment upon the diagram, and by the observation of the diagram, so modified, ascertains the truth

FIGURE 2.3 *The rabbit that is also a duck: Joseph Jastrow's duck-rabbit picture.*[10]

of the conclusion" (id.). The proof given before that the sum of the three angles of a triangle equals two right angles, is an example of theorematic deduction. Since in theorematic deduction free acts are performed upon a diagram, the same conclusion can often be reached in multiple ways. In corollarial deduction there is no such variety—one can only see what is there or fail to do so. Though merely looking at a diagram can yield surprise, as when we discover that a picture of a rabbit is also a picture of a duck, theorematic deduction is the true source of surprise in mathematical reasoning.

An important mathematical operation, one that furnishes much of the material for the hypothetical states of things studied by mathematicians, is abstraction. Peirce distinguishes two operations of thought to which the term abstraction is generally applied. First, there is the situation where we concentrate our attention on one feature of something to the neglect of others. We do this when in buying a couch we focus on its color, while neglecting its size, style, comfort, etc. Peirce calls this prescissive abstraction or *prescission* (CP4.235). Thus, in geometry we *prescind* shape from color (CP5.449). Peirce distinguishes prescission from what he calls hypostatic abstraction. By this he means the creation of an *ens rationis,* or object of reason, from nonsubstantive thought (id.). In hypostatic abstraction, a thought about a subject is made itself a subject of thought, and thus it can become an independent subject of discourse (CP5.534). We do this when we move from the adjective "virtuous" to the noun "virtue" and then proceed to develop a theory of virtues. For Peirce, the construction of objects of thought through hypostatic abstraction is essential to mathematics:

> In order to get an inkling—though a very slight one—of the importance of this operation in mathematics, it will suffice to remember that a collection is an hypostatic abstraction, or *ens rationis,* that multitude is the hypostatic abstraction derived from a predicate of a collection, and that a cardinal number is an abstraction attached to a multitude. So an ordinal number is an abstraction attached to a place, which in its turn is a hypostatic abstraction from a relative character of a unit of a series, itself an abstraction again. (CP5.534)

In brief, in hypostatic abstraction we extract a certain aspect from a hypothetical state of things and make it an independent object of thought of which other things can subsequently be predicated. Peirce considers the discovery of powerful abstractions a difficult art, and finding the right abstraction often initiates an enormous mathematical advance. From what has been said it should also be clear that such hypostatical abstractions are more than mere products of the imagination of a singular individual. I return to this in Chapter 8.

In his 1673 Comédie-ballet, *Le malade imaginaire* Molière famously ridiculed hypostatic abstraction by having a medical student solemnly declare that opium puts people to sleep because of its "dormative power." But even that is not useless, says Peirce, as it allows us to study this power in its own right, which opens up the possibility of finding it in other substances besides opium.

The most challenging part in mathematical reasoning, however, is not deduction or abstraction, but generalization. For Peirce this is the true engine of mathematics. Strictly speaking a generalized model reverts back to what it is generalized from by imposing a limitation. Thus, non-Euclidean geometries are generalizations of Euclidean geometry of which the latter becomes a special case where the parallel postulate is invoked as an added limitation. One mechanism for finding generalized models is by examining extreme (or degenerate) cases. For instance, the definition of a triangle given above allows for the extreme case of one of the angles being zero. Examination of this shows that even three points on a line constitute a triangle—and one for which the sum of its interior angles equal two right angles. This leads to a broader conception of a triangle of which our familiar conception is a special case that is characterized by the added limitation that its three-angle points may not lie on a single line.

In sum, for Peirce, mathematical reasoning includes much more than giving proofs. Reducing mathematics to demonstration, as Peirce sees Euclid do in the *Elements,* leaves out the most important aspects of mathematical reasoning: construction, observation, experiment, abstraction, and generalization. Demonstration, Peirce writes to his brother, is only "the pavement over which the mathematician drives his team, with a goal in view and with a plan for reaching it."[11]

As we will see more clearly later, this rather longish detour through mathematics is crucial to understanding philosophy, as philosophers often depend upon mathematical argumentation and are often eager to utilize the *entia rationis* that mathematicians abstracted.

2.4 Mathematics, philosophy, and logic

In our brief discussion of Kant we saw that he believes that philosophers should shun mathematical reasoning. Peirce opines otherwise. Not only has philosophy much to learn from mathematics, but even the syllogisms, which Kant considers a paradigm case of discursive reasoning, are for Peirce a form of mathematical and hence diagrammatic reasoning. In line with this, Peirce observes that what characterizes a good style of philosophizing is that it "approximates as closely as possible to a self-explaining diagram or a tabular array of familiar symbols" (CN3:129). It is not merely how mathematicians reason that is of use to the philosopher, but several mathematical conceptions, such as the infinite, infinitesimals, collections, multitudes, and continuity come to play an important role in philosophy as well, including Peirce's. Some of these will be discussed in the chapters that follow. This does not mean that mathematicians are naturally good philosophers. In fact, the situation is quite the opposite. And as we will see, philosophy requires very different powers than those that make a great mathematician.

A few words should be said about the relation between mathematics and logic, especially given the mathematization of logic during Peirce's life and his own contributions thereto. A popular take on the relation between the two is *logicism*: the view that mathematics can ultimately be grounded in, reduced to, or deduced from something like "the laws of logic." Historically, logicism follows in the footsteps of Pythagoreanism, the long-standing attempt by mathematicians to ground all mathematics in number (i.e. in arithmetic). Since Boole developed his new algebra of logic as an arithmetic, the idea that mathematics can be grounded in logic—that is, in a Boolean type algebra—comes down to a natural extension of the Pythagorean ideal. In Peirce's time the main proponent of the logicist stance is Richard Dedekind, with whose work Peirce is quite familiar.

With regard to logicism, we should distinguish between two very different claims. The first is that the science of mathematics can be grounded in the science of logic. As is evident from Peirce's division of the sciences in Chapter 1, Peirce is not a logicist in this way. Mathematics and logic are for him very different enterprises. Whereas mathematics is confined to the study of hypothetical states of things, logic resides under the positive sciences as the study of how we *should* reason if we want to gain knowledge about the world (Section 4.1).

The second claim is whether all mathematics (all of it, or only arithmetic) can be grounded in, reduced to, or deduced from a single branch *within* mathematics, and if so, whether this single branch can be justifiably identified as (mathematical) logic. The above account of Peirce's mathematics suggests that he is not a logicist in this sense either. As we saw there is much more to mathematical reasoning than mere demonstration in the rather limited sense logicists typically take it to be. However, to get a better sense of Peirce's position it may be helpful to see how Peirce subdivides mathematics, and examine how the various parts relate.

Mathematics can be divided several ways. The traditional division is between algebra and geometry. This is essentially a division according to method, or, more accurately, according to types of schemata used: "linear figures with letters attached" for geometry, and "arrays of characters . . . with which are associated certain rules of permissible transformation" for algebra (CP4.246). Peirce rejects this way of dividing mathematics because either method can be applied to any mathematical subject, and sometimes the most fruitful approach is to combine them. Taking seriously his definition of mathematics and what it entails, Peirce proposes to divide mathematics in terms of the ideal systems, or hypotheses, that mathematicians study. Peirce first groups these hypotheses by the number of elements that are supposed, and then divides them further according to what kind of relations between these elements is the focus of the hypothesis. The result is a distinction in three types of systems: finite collections, infinite collections, and true continua (CP1.283). The first can be further divided into those that contain only two elements and those containing a finite number of elements greater than two. The basis of this, at first sight rather odd division, is discussed in the next chapter when we look at Peirce's doctrine of the categories. For systems of infinite collections Peirce distinguishes between arithmetic and calculus. Finally, topical geometry, a discipline that in Peirce's day is still very much in its infancy, treats of true continua.

Hypotheses containing only two elements are the simplest in that there can be no hypotheses that have fewer elements than two:

> Were nothing at all supposed, mathematics would have no ground at all to go upon. Were the hypothesis merely that there was nothing but one unit, there would not be a possibility of a

question, since only one answer would be possible. Consequently, the simplest possible hypothesis is that there are two objects, which we may denote by v and f. (CP4.250)

Such dichotomic algebras allow for questions such as the following: If we have a certain unknown object x to which the hypothesis is taken to apply, is x v or is it f? If we have three unknown objects, x, y, and z, all of which are v, would x or y remain v when z changes to f?

Peirce mentions ethics and logic (albeit not all logic) as applications of dichotomic algebra: "This [is] the system of evaluation which ethics applies to actions in dividing them into the right and the wrong, and which non-relative logic applies to assertions in dividing them into the true and the false" (CP4.368). Peirce continues by observing that this type of mathematics "amounts to very little," and that "those who seek to make a calculus of the algebra of logic struggle vainly after mathematical interest by complicating their problems" (id.).

Now, whether Peirce is a logicist in the second sense would depend on something like the following: whether all mathematics (i.e. all hypotheses dealing with finite or infinite collections, and all hypotheses dealing with true continua) can be reduced to a single dichotomic algebra in which each element has a value of either v or f, and in which the rules of transformation are restricted in such a manner that v can never lead to f. This would be a logicism of the strictest form to which subsequent concessions could possibly be made should it prove too narrow (either by broadening what is meant by logic, most significantly by bringing in the logic of relatives, or by lifting the requirement that it applies to all mathematics). Logicism thus interpreted expresses some sort of foundationalism with regard to the ideal states of things mathematicians construct and study: ideally they can all be inferred from a single hypothetical system of dichotomic algebra, which is the simplest mathematics that can be conceived. Given Peirce's conception of mathematics, the claim that this can be done, even if only in principle, is at best highly speculative.

CHAPTER THREE

Phenomenology and the categories

In the previous chapter, we saw that Peirce rejects the received opinion that mathematics, because of its abstractness, and hence its general applicability, is the most basic of the positive sciences. In fact, Peirce even denies that mathematics is a positive science at all. A positive science, as Peirce defines it, is a science that seeks to affirm or deny something of some subject, as with "John's trousers are green," "Atoms are divisible," or "Not all birds can fly." Mathematics, for Peirce, does not aim to do this. Mathematicians study only conditional or hypothetical propositions, making it altogether irrelevant whether what they study actually represents anything. As our brief discussion of mathematics in the previous chapter has shown, declaring mathematics a positive science not only misconstrues what mathematics is really about, but also severely restricts what mathematicians can legitimately do.

Instead of mathematics, Peirce makes philosophy the most basic of the positive sciences. Philosophy, he writes, "contends itself with a more attentive scrutiny and comparison of the facts of everyday life, such as present themselves to every adult and sane person, and for the most part in every day and hour of his waking life" (EP2:146). To engage in philosophy, we need no special equipment like telescopes or particle accelerators, nor need we possess any specialized background knowledge, as with, say, forensic pathology or cultural anthropology. The aim of philosophy is to provide us with a *Weltanschauung*—a general way of apprehending and interpreting the universe that can function as the general backdrop for our thoughts about the world, including any pronouncements of the special sciences (EP2:146f). Though philosophy comes first in Peirce's division of the positive sciences, he does not consider it as an autonomous discipline characterized by procedures that are different from those used in the sciences. In Peirce's view, there is no such separation between philosophy and science. What distinguishes the philosopher is that he makes these "facts of every day life" the sole subject of his study, rather than taking them, often without much reflection, as the springboard for certain specialized observations, as does the typical scientist. A different way to cast the distinction is to say that philosophy (or *cenoscopy*, as Peirce also calls it, borrowing the term from Bentham) "is founded upon the common experience of all men," whereas in the special sciences, or *idioscopy*, one "discovers new phenomena" (CP8.19). It should be noted further that Peirce's conception of science is much broader than what is common today, especially among English-speaking philosophers. I return to this in Section 6.3.

Peirce divides philosophy into three branches. The most basic is phenomenology, or *phaneroscopy* as he prefers to call it. Its sole task is, "to draw up an inventory of appearances without going into any investigation of their truth" (CP2.120). Next comes the normative sciences, which study how these phenomena relate to certain ends. Peirce distinguishes three normative sciences: esthetics, ethics, and logic. The third and final branch of philosophy is metaphysics, which studies "the most general features of reality and real objects" (EP2:375). Metaphysics is that part of philosophy that seeks to construct the *Weltanschauung* that I just mentioned. Each subsequent branch or sub-branch derives part of its principles from those that precede it in the division, and all utilize mathematics.

In the current chapter, I discuss Peirce's phenomenology. More detailed discussions of logic (broadly interpreted as the theory of how to reason) and metaphysics are found in subsequent chapters.

3.1 Phenomenology

When explaining what philosophy is, Peirce typically begins with logic, which he defines as the (normative) theory of how we should reason if we want to preserve truth. Peirce then moves backwards, arguing that logic thus defined presupposes the normative science of ethics, which is the study of self-controlled, or deliberate, conduct in general. Next he argues that ethics presupposes an even more basic normative science, called esthetics, which he takes to be the study of what is most admirable in and of itself, that is, independently of any ulterior reason (both ethics and logic, bring in an ulterior reason). Esthetics, in turn, depends on a science that merely contemplates phenomena as they appear without making any judgment about what ought or ought not to be, describe them as they are encountered, and see whether any regularity or structure reveals itself. This last science Peirce calls phenomenology, and he contends that there can be no positive science more basic than this. In this section, I discuss what phenomenology studies, what it aims to achieve, why it is basic, and why Peirce prefers the term phaneroscopy. In the next section, I discuss Peirce's phenomenological derivation of the categories.

Peirce's concern for proper terminology (Section 1.4) causes him to entertain various names for this basic science, including phenomenology, phanerochemy, phaneroscopy, categorics, empirics, and phenoscopy. Though he uses the term phenomenology rather extensively, he later rejects it and gives good reasons for doing so.[1] Peirce prefers the term phaneroscopy, which derives from the Greek *phaneron* (what is visible or manifest) and *skopein* (to view). Phaneroscopy thus becomes "the description of the *phaneron*" (CP1.284). Peirce defines the phaneron as: "the *collective total* of all that is in any way or in any sense present to the mind, quite regardless of whether it corresponds to any real thing or not" (id.; emphasis added). Elsewhere he similarly defines the phaneron as:

> the *total content* of any one consciousness (for any one is substantially any other), the sum of all we have in mind in any way whatever, regardless of its cognitive value. This is pretty vague: I intentionally leave it so. I will only point out that I do not limit the reference to an instantaneous state of consciousness; for the clause "in any way whatever" takes in memory and all habitual cognition. (EP2:362; emphasis added)

Both passages indicate that the phaneron enters consciousness as an all-encompassing totality. To argue that what enters consciousness is a *plurality* of phanerons (as is common for instance with those who take sense impressions as basic) already brings in acts of the understanding (not to speak of certain developed theories of cognition) as any reference to a plurality already implies making discriminations within the totality that manifests itself.

To better understand what Peirce means by phaneron let us look at some competing terms and see why Peirce rejects them. Peirce rejects *phenomenon*, in part to distance himself from Hegel's *Phenomenology*, but also to avoid confusion with how the term is used in physics where it stands for certain perceived regularities that can be made the subject of scientific description and explanation, such as the appearance of electrical sparks when combing your hair in cold dry weather.

Peirce also rejects William James' *pure experience*, experience that is free from any conceptualizing, which James describes as "a mere motley which we have to unify by our wits"[2] not unlike the newborn's first encounter with the world when it "feels it all as one great blooming, buzzing confusion."[3] Peirce's main reason for rejecting James' notion is that it is too limiting: "*experience* is what life has forced upon us,—a vague idea no doubt. But my *phaneron* is not limited to what is *forced* upon us; it also embraces all that we most capriciously conjure up" (NEM3:834).[4]

Peirce further rejects the empiricists' notion of *idea*. In his *Essay concerning Human Understanding*, Locke defines *idea* as "whatsoever is the Object of the Understanding when a Man thinks," and adds that he uses it "to express whatever is meant by *Phantasm, Notion, Species,* or whatever it is, which the Mind can be employ'd about in thinking."[5] The similarity with the phaneron is clear, as Peirce himself admits (CP1.285). Moreover, by including phantasms and notions, Locke avoids the limitation Peirce saw in James' concept of "pure experience." As Peirce sees it, however, the term phaneron has several advantages above that of idea. It avoids the troublesome ambiguity of *idea*, which can be either an object of thought or the thought itself. It moreover avoids any connotation with attention—singling something out at the expense of whatever else may be present in consciousness, as when we say we have an idea of a mountain ridge. And it avoids contamination with how the meaning of the term evolved thanks to the British empiricists who made ideas the abstract building blocks of knowledge. Consequently, using the term idea would introduce into phaneroscopy all sorts of connotations and preconceptions that are better kept at bay. For similar reasons, Peirce would have rejected the twentieth-century notion of sense data advanced by Bertrand Russell and others.

Peirce's conception of the phaneron further resonates what decades earlier in "A New List of Categories" he calls "the present in general"—that is, the present before any comparison or discrimination is made (W2:49). Peirce called this present in general also the "it" and "substance" (id.).

Having thus defined the phaneron and identified phaneroscopy as the science of the phaneron, the question becomes: what is the aim of this phaneroscopy? Peirce's answer is that for phaneroscopy to form a basis for the positive sciences of discovery it must provide some sort of inventory of the elements that are often or even universally present in the phaneron—an inventory the other sciences can subsequently build upon. These elements, or ingredients as Peirce also calls them, are the most basic elements of all cognition, and given how Peirce defines the phaneron, this also includes all that is created by the mind, including mathematical objects.[6] The reason for this is that "no things whatever can differ more from one another than ingredients of the phaneron may differ; since whatever we at all know we must know through ingredients of the phaneron" (R477:10). Peirce next follows Aristotle in calling those things "which are so utterly disparate as to have nothing in common," categories (id.), and he even goes so far as to call phaneroscopy "the Doctrine of Categories" (CP2.120) and categorics (RL75). In brief, the aim of phaneroscopy is to draw up a catalog of the categories.

Before saying anything more, we do well to recall that in phaneroscopy we do not seek to determine what is true of the phaneron, or to determine what is real and what is not. Were we to do that, we would be grounding phaneroscopy in logic or in metaphysics, and that is exactly the opposite of what we seek to establish. Hence, the phaneroscopist must avoid taking the phaneron to represent anything, or look at it with any preestablished purpose in mind. Phaneroscopy, as Peirce defines it, concerns only what seems, and on that premise it seeks to describe "the essentially different elements which seem to present themselves in what seems" (CP2.197). Finding these different elements, Peirce argues, requires a way of thinking that is very different from what we find elsewhere in philosophy, in mathematics, or in the special sciences. They cannot be a product of reasoning, as what characterizes reasoning is that it maintains the truth of its conclusions even if the way things seem is wholly contrary to them. Consequently, the application of reasoning, even apart from grounding phaneroscopy in a science that is in turn grounded in it, brings us clearly outside the realm of phaneroscopy, as in phaneroscopy there can be no other assertions than that there are certain seemings within which there seem to be certain recurring elements.

If the phaneroscopist cannot provide reasons or arguments, what is the phaneroscopist to do? One way of looking at this is to compare the phaneroscopist with the seasoned mountain climber who meets a novice who wants to climb to the peak of a mountain. He can give the novice directions and hope for the best, or he can accompany him and coach him all the way up. To reach the peak, though, the novice has no choice but to make the climb himself. Similarly, the phaneroscopist can give directions—tell the reader where to look and what to expect—but the actual observation each must do for oneself and each must on the basis of it evaluate the phaneroscopist's account.

Of course, not everyone needs to climb mountains, nor is everyone equally fit for it. The same, Peirce argues, is true for phaneroscopy. In his second Harvard Lecture of 1903, Peirce distinguishes three faculties we need to possess (or acquire) before engaging in phaneroscopy. The first and most important one is "the faculty of seeing what stares one in the face, just as it presents itself, unreplaced by any interpretation, unsophisticated by any allowance for this or for that supposed modifying circumstance" (EP2:147). This is the observational power of the artist who has trained herself to see things unencumbered by how they are supposed to look. To the artist, Peirce explains, snow is seldom if ever white—as convention says it is—but it is of a dull blue in the shadow, a rich yellow in the sunshine, etc. The second faculty we need is more characteristic of the hunter than the artist. We must acquire "a resolute discrimination which fastens itself like a bulldog upon the particular feature that we are studying, follows it wherever it may lurk, and detects it beneath all its disguises" (id.). The third faculty is "the generalizing power of the mathematician who produces the abstract formula that comprehends the very essence of the feature under examination purified from all admixture of extraneous and irrelevant accompaniments" (id.).

Phaneroscopy, as Peirce defines it, involves the search for the main ingredients of the phaneron, or the categories. In the next section, I provide a short phaneroscopic primer on how to extract these categories from the phaneron.

3.2 Derivation of the categories

In the previous section, we saw that the task before us is to draw up a catalogue of categories. In addition to merely identifying the different categories, we must also (1) "make out the characteristics of each," (2) "show the relations of each to the others," and for the catalogue as a whole (3) "prove its sufficiency and freedom from redundancies" (CP5.43).

Peirce first draws a distinction between universal and particular categories. The former, he explains, would "belong to every phenomenon, one being perhaps more prominent in one aspect of that phenomenon than another but all of them belonging to every phenomenon," and it is these that he sets out to find (id.). The task is an ambitious one. We must look for those characteristics that are never wanting in the phaneron, no matter whether it is "something that outward experience forces upon our attention, or whether it be the wildest of dreams, or whether it be the most abstract and general of the conclusions of science" (CP5.41). Moreover, since we seek to draw up a catalogue free from redundancies, we should look for those elements that are indecomposable, so that we do not end up including categories that can be reduced to combinations of simpler ones.

Since we are seeking to extract or separate something from the phaneron, and make it an object of thought, we should first become clear about what we mean by separation. Peirce distinguishes three grades of separation that are often run together: dissociation, prescission (or abstraction), and discrimination (or distinction). We can *dissociate* two ideas when they are "so little allied that one of them may be present to the consciousness in an image which does not contain the other at all" (W5:238). Thus, we can *dissociate* sound from melody, but not melody from sound. This is because we can *imagine* sound without melody, but Peirce argues, we cannot imagine melody without sound. However, in cases where we cannot dissociate two things, we can still *suppose* them separate. This is what Peirce calls *prescission*. The idea is that whereas we cannot dissociate, say, color from space (because we can have no *image* of an uncolored space), we can still *suppose* an uncolored space by prescinding space from color. Similarly, we can prescind melody from sound. We can even represent melody without any reference to sound at all, as we do in a musical score. In prescission, we focus on one element to the neglect of all others. Finally, we can *discriminate* two things, even when we cannot dissociate or prescind them. That is to say, when we cannot even suppose two things to be separated we may still be able to distinguish them. Thus, though we can prescind space from color to form uncolored space, we cannot prescind color from space to form non-extended color. However, to even say that we cannot do so requires that we can discriminate, or distinguish, color from space. Hence, when we are extracting the categories from the phaneron we must make explicit what grade of separation we are talking about: is it dissociation, prescission, or mere discrimination?

Peirce distinguishes two ways we can search for the universal categories: according to matter and according to form or structure. Peirce attempts both and eventually settles for the latter (CP1.288). Since phaneroscopy is to be the basis of the positive sciences, the latter is also the most fruitful. Moreover, it puts us in a better position to utilize mathematics. Since we are looking for the *indecomposable* parts of the phaneron, Peirce further observes that, "no mode of division of them can be more important than that according to the degrees of complexity of their combinations," and he draws a comparison with the division of chemical elements according to their valency (NEM3:834).

Having determined that the next order of business is to discover the different ways the indecomposable elements of the phaneron can be combined, we can ask the mathematician to develop a model and see whether we can apply it to the phaneron. The question we are asking is the following: Can we identify a limited set of indecomposable elements that would allow us to create any conceivable complexity, and what do those elements look like in terms of the composition relations they can enter into?

To answer this question, Peirce uses the method of graphs. In this method, which originated in chemistry and which had recently been introduced into mathematics, a system of dots and lines is set up such that it can represent any relationship. Now what are the indecomposable elements of such a system? Intuitively one would say: dots and lines. So let us begin by putting a single black dot on a white sheet of paper and say that this isolated dot represents what it is unrelated to anything else. Peirce calls this a first and he uses the term *firstness* to denote the character of being a first. In this manner, we obtain as our first universal category "the mode of being of that which is such as it is, positively and without reference to anything else" (CP8.328).

However, by putting even a single dot on a sheet of paper we divide that sheet into two, one part being white and the other black. Hence, Peirce continues, one cannot represent the idea of a first without immediately introducing the idea of something else—that is, a second. This does not mean, Peirce explains, "that *one* logically involves *two* as a part of its conception; but that to realize *one* (even if only in thought), some *second* must be used" (R915:4).[7] Peirce thus arrives at his second category, which he calls *secondness*: "the mode of being of that which is such as it is, with respect to a second but regardless of any third" (CP8.328).

In the method of graphs, we can make this notion of a second that we are forced to introduce more explicit by putting two dots on the sheet and connect them with a line. However, more careful observation shows that the line is superfluous as the sheet already connects the dots. As Peirce generalizes the point: "in the method of graphs every pair of dots is to be conceived as connected by one kind or another; for to leave a pair unjoined is to represent them as joined in a another way" (R915:4). What this means is that two dots cannot be represented without a medium of some sort, that is, without something connecting the two. Again, this does not mean that *two* logically involves *three* as part of its conception, but that in order to realize *two* (even if only in thought) some *third* must be involved. This brings Peirce to his third category, which he names *thirdness,* and by which he means "the mode of being of that which is such as it is, in bringing a second and third into relation to each other" (CP8.328).

Now can we think of *three* without having to bring in a *fourth*? The method of graphs again shows us the answer. Let us put three dots on the paper and connect them with lines just as we did earlier with the two dots (see Figure 3.1). Next recall that we are looking for indecomposable elements, which means that we may not accept as a fourth category anything that can be reduced to the first three.

FIGURE 3.1 *Graphical proof of Peirce's theorem.*

It is here that the generalizing ability of the mathematician comes in handy. First we remove the three lines and let the three dots be unjoined (that is, let the sheet, or our thought, be what connects them). Next we substitute a line for one of the dots. Shifting the elements around subsequently allows us two represent both dots as being connected by the line (thus removing the need of the sheet or our thought to connect them). That we can reduce the diagram this way shows that no fourth category is needed.

The conclusion that these are the only three categories, that they cannot be reduced to one another, and that any fourth category can be reduced to them, is called Peirce's theorem. The theorem states that it is impossible to define triadic relations in terms of simpler ones (e.g. dyads), and that all relations with four or more relata can be reduced to simpler ones. The above argument also shows that all three categories, as they are present even in an isolated dot, are always present.

At this point, we should return to our discussion of separation. Our analysis shows that although we can *discriminate* the three categories, we clearly cannot *dissociate* them. The case of the single dot shows that we cannot imagine anything that does not involve all three categories. However, the above analysis also shows that we can *prescind* firstness from both secondness and thirdness, and that we can prescind secondness from thirdness. That is to say, we can extract them from the diagram as *entia rationis* that in turn can be made into separate objects of discourse (Section 2.3). The above analysis further reveals that we *cannot* prescind firstness from secondness, as no second is possible without a first to which it is second, and that thirdness cannot be prescinded from firstness and secondness, as thirdness is a mediation between two. All we can do is to discriminate them.

Our charge was to identify the different categories, make out their characteristics, show their interrelations, and prove that our list is both sufficient and free from redundancy. Our application of the method of graphs establishes all of this. We must keep in mind, though, that all we have done so far is to give a *mathematical* model, and that we still have to apply it to the phaneron. In doing so, let's take a very simple example, designed to bring out the three categories in isolation, so that their nature and interrelations stand out as clearly as we can get them. In a sense we are asking for the impossible, as the categories we are looking for are supposed to be universal; that is to say, they must all be present in all that comes before the mind, and this precludes that we can dissociate them. The best we can do is to imagine something that approaches the experience of each category in isolation so we can get an idea of them as phaneroscopic categories.

To grasp firstness as a phaneroscopic category, imagine the wholly self-effacing experience of floating in a hot air balloon high above the ocean in a perfectly still dense fog.[8] There is nothing else, we are not even aware of ourselves as being present; we are, so to say, one with the fog. Of course, in describing this situation the three categories jump out immediately, as we have a balloonist, the dense fog, and a connection between the two. It is not, however, the *description* of the experience that we are interested in, but *the experience itself;* and all we are claiming is that the category of firstness dominates the experience. Now imagine that the perfect stillness that encapsulates the balloonist is suddenly broken by a loud and persistent hiss. This brings in a second, and as the balloonist has no idea what causes it, or how it relates to the experience he had, this second manifests itself as pure intrusion. Peirce also gives the example of someone wandering through town, daydreaming and wholly oblivious of his surroundings, and who is suddenly struck against the back of the head with a heavy beam. Here too, what enters as a second is unmediated otherness. Thirdness comes on the scene when the balloonist comes to realize that the loud hissing is caused by a rapid escape of air from the balloon above him, possibly caused by a rip in the fabric. In the balloonist's confusion and the slow but awful realization as to the origin of the sound, we see the emergence of mediation, or thirdness, as a category separate from both firstness and secondness.

The unfortunate adventure of the balloonist gives us an idea of what the phaneroscopic categories look like. Moreover, as some experimentation with our thought example quickly reveals, it confirms the relations between them that our mathematical model brought out. We can prescind firstness from secondness, and thirdness from the other two, but not secondness from firstness, etc. There are still tough questions to be answered, but in the end they all come down to the following: How well does our mathematical model apply to the phaneron, no matter what that phaneron may be? In a sense this is an open-ended empirical question, as one never knows what strange phenomena we may encounter. Peirce claims that he has looked long and hard trying to disprove his doctrine of the three categories but that he has never found anything that contradicted it, and he extends to everyone the invitation to do the same. Put differently, strong inductive evidence that the doctrine of the three categories is correct is easily obtained and this allows us to say that, at least from a pragmatic and scientific standpoint, the burden of proof lies on those who reject the doctrine.

Before continuing our discussion of the phaneroscopic categories, let's first take a step back and perform the mathematician's trick of looking at degenerate cases. As we saw in Chapter 2, a study of such cases can prove most valuable in increasing our understanding of what we are dealing with. To recall, in mathematics a degenerate case is one where the value for one or more of the variables or constants equals or approaches zero or infinite. Thus $x^2 = 0$ and $y^2 = 0$ are degenerate forms of the quadratic equation $x^2 + 2xy + y^2 = 0$.

For Peirce, there can be no degenerate firsts. However, he distinguishes one type of degenerate seconds and two types of degenerate thirds. Genuine secondness is truly external. It is a direct pairing or opposition in fact. Degenerate secondness, in contrast, is a product of some internal relation or other. When I shout someone's name and its echo startles me, what startles me is not a genuine intrusion of otherness, because the echo was caused by my own shout. There is secondness, but it is secondness of a degenerate kind. Other examples of degenerate secondness are the relation of identity (Julius Caesar rules with Julius Caesar), and the sudden realization of a man that he is stubborn.

A genuine third mediates between objects through a character that would disappear if one of the objects it mediates between were to be removed. A comparison of two objects is a good example of a genuine third. Were one of the objects removed the comparison disappears as well. Peirce distinguishes two types of degenerate thirds. The first mediates between objects through two separate relations, one of which it would lose when one object were to be removed, the other when the other object were to be removed.

A safety pin holding together two pieces of fabric exemplifies this kind of degenerate thirdness. Were we to remove one piece of fabric, this does not affect the relation between the safety pin and the other piece of fabric. The second type of a degenerate third mediates between objects through a character it continues to have even if *both* the objects between which it mediates would cease to exist. For instance, the city of Paris lies intermediate between Madrid and Amsterdam in virtue of its geographical position, and this position it continues to have even when the two other cities are destroyed.

Peirce begins his search for the categories in the 1860s and it is helpful to look briefly at this, in part because of what it reveals about the origin of Peirce's list of categories, and in part because of what it reveals about what Peirce sought to establish early on. Peirce's search for the categories originates in his youthful and extensive study of Kant's *Critique* of Pure Reason, and culminates in his 1867 "On a New List of Categories" (W2:49–58). Like Kant, Peirce acknowledges the need of reducing the manifold of sense impressions to some sort of comprehensible unity. We do so, Peirce argues, still following Kant, by conceptualizing. Hence, Peirce seeks to determine how we can extract propositional knowledge—which he identifies with *being*—from the multiplicity of non-conceptualized sense impressions, which he calls *substance*. It should be said that the conception of being that is here introduced is strictly confined to what is implied in the copula of a proposition, as in "All centaurs *are* cloven hoofed," and nothing more. We should avoid introducing any metaphysical associations we have with the term. As Peirce explains: "Substance and being are the two poles of thought. Substance is the beginning, being the *end* of all conception. Substance is inapplicable to a predicate, being is equally so to a subject" (W1:518).

In the *Critique of Pure Reason,* Kant based his categories on formal logic. Doing so, Kant believed, ensured a lasting foundation, as logic had not really changed since Aristotle. Because Kant sought to keep the categories wholly a priori, he rejected experience as a source. The discovery of Kant's method, and the realization that it made Kant's metaphysical system spring out of his logic, causes Peirce to realize the importance of logic, and a subject worthy of devoting his life to. Peirce's study of logic, however, quickly reveals that Kant's use of logic had been quite superficial, and Peirce's own search for the categories becomes an attempt to remedy this.

Rejecting Kant's stark separation between the empirical and the a priori, Peirce does not confine himself merely to a logical dissection of the proposition, as Kant had done, but he extracts the categories from an examination of the phenomenon—an examination that is non-psychological and prelogical. Returning to the phenomena (substance, or the phaneron) distinguishes Peirce's derivation of the categories from previous attempts. "My list differs from those of Aristotle, Kant, and Hegel," Peirce later observes, "in that they never really went back to examining the Phenomenon to see what was to be observed there.... They simply took current conceptions and arranged them" (NEM4:19).

To recapitulate, according to Peirce three, and only three, categories present themselves in all that comes before the mind—no matter whether we speak of the most vivid sense impression or the faintest flight of fancy—and he calls them firstness, secondness, and thirdness. They are, first, the pure quality of being what it is, positively, and independently of anything else; second, the unmediated opposition of a first to something it is not; and third, a positive relation between two firsts that are second to each other. Reminiscent of the ongoing Pythagoreanism in mathematics (the attempt to reduce geometry to arithmetic; see Section 2.4), Peirce also calls them the cenopythagorean categories, where the prefix *ceno* echoes at once the Greek *kainos* (new) and *koinos* (common). At one point Peirce even reads them into the first three numbers of the Pythagorean decad: "*One* was the origin; *two*, stalwart resistance; *three*, mediation and beauty."[9] Elsewhere Peirce refers to them as the Protean categories, after Proteus the Greek sea god who can foretell the future but who constantly changes his shape to avoid that he has to, so that he only answers those who can catch him. The same is true for the categories. They too appear in countless guises and are often hard to discern. This is all but to be expected as they universally apply to anything we can possibly think of, whether it is a toothache, the spatial relations of a twelve-dimensional hypercube, a conflict of values, Hamlet's relation to Shakespeare, a paradigm shift, or the determination of guilt in a criminal case.

CHAPTER FOUR

The normative science of logic

In Chapter 3, we examined Peirce's phenomenology and his derivation of the categories. In this chapter, we look at normative science, which comes second in Peirce's threefold division of philosophy. Peirce divides normative science into esthetics, ethics, and logic. Peirce realizes fairly late in life that logic is a normative enterprise that depends heavily on ethics, and it is even later when he realizes that ethics depends heavily on esthetics. The phrase normative science—as well as its division into esthetics, ethics, and logic—originates in Friedrich Überweg's 1857 *System der Logik*, a book Peirce was quite impressed with. In spite of the central importance of the normative sciences, Peirce does not see himself as having much to contribute to either esthetics or ethics, and it is primarily the need to ground logic that causes him to discuss both disciplines. What Peirce aims for is a discussion of esthetics and ethics as sciences of discovery. He even considers them the "most purely theoretical of purely theoretical sciences" (CP1.281).

At first glance it may strike one as odd that Peirce includes the normative sciences among the positive sciences, as the latter seek to tell us strictly what is, whereas the former seek to tell us what ought to be, no matter how things are. However, to exclude the normative sciences from the positive sciences on this basis uses a far narrower conception of positive science than that with which we began. Recall that the positive sciences were defined as those that seek to declare the truth of categorical propositions—that is, propositions that positively affirm or deny something of some subject. At least prima facie this applies equally to normative statements, such as "Thou shall not kill" or "Michelangelo's David is beautiful." Including such propositions conflicts with a prevalent conception of positive science that restricts its domain to that of existing things only—a view that is found among philosophers whom Peirce calls nominalists. However, nominalism, like its rival realism, is a *metaphysical* position regarding truth and reality. Strictly, metaphysical viewpoints cannot have any bearing upon the argument here, and this includes metaphysically inspired nominalistic strictures on what constitutes science and what does not. True, if when developing the normative sciences we find ourselves committed to metaphysical views that are sufficiently absurd to constitute a *reductio*, this will show our conception of normative science untenable, but that only tells us that we have to start all over again; it is not an open invitation to introduce metaphysical conceptions when developing phenomenology and normative science. I will return to Peirce's metaphysics, and the debate between nominalists and realists, in Chapter 8.

Peirce briefly considers ranking the normative science under mathematics, if only because "its reasoning is mostly mathematical" (EP2:147). Peirce rejects this option, not only because its deductions lack the purity of mathematical arguments, but also because the three normative sciences are "intended to conform to positive truth of fact and . . . derive their interest from that circumstance almost exclusively" (CP5.126). However, we can use the doctrine of the categories developed in the previous chapter to situate and structure normative science. Whereas phenomenology studies phenomena without any reference to anything else, or in their firstness, normative science studies phenomena in relation to certain ends, that is, in their secondness. It is, as Peirce puts it, "the science of the laws of conformity of things to ends" (CP5.129). Metaphysics, the third branch of philosophy, studies phenomena insofar as they are subject to law or thirdness.

Taking his cues from Überweg, Peirce divides normative science into esthetics, ethics, and logic, the respective ends of which are traditionally identified as beauty, goodness, and truth. Once again applying the doctrine of the categories, Peirce proceeds by saying that esthetics studies its end simply as it presents itself (or in its firstness), ethics studies its end as it relates to action or efforts of will (or in its secondness), and logic studies its end in regard to representation (or in its thirdness).[1] Peirce devotes practically all his time to logic, or the theory of how we *should* reason when we want our arguments to preserve truth. Esthetics and ethics pretty much enter the scene only insofar they are needed to provide a basis for the normative science of logic; that is, insofar they constitute a bridge between phenomenology and logic. Consequently, before discussing logic proper, I discuss esthetics and ethics, together with how they relate to phenomenology on the one side and logic on the other. The remainder of the chapter is devoted to logic.

4.1 Grounding logic in ethics and esthetics

In justifying his classification of philosophy, Peirce generally begins with logic, the discipline he is most familiar with, and then shows how logic depends on ethics, ethics on esthetics, and esthetics on phenomenology. So we best begin by asking how Peirce sees logic. Especially since Peirce did much work in mathematical logic, this also raises the question how logic relates to mathematics. For our current purpose it suffices to say that Peirce considers logic a positive science, which means that it can be made a subject of mathematical models in the manner described in Chapter 2. In this sense, logic is not different from physics, chemistry, or economics. Mathematical logic, then, concerns the creation, development, and study of these models.

Peirce describes the positive science of logic as: "the theory of *right* reasoning, of what reasoning ought to be, not of what it is" (CP2.3). This presupposes that we can distinguish good reasoning from bad reasoning and that we should aim for the former while avoiding the latter.[2] Logic, for Peirce, is thus a normative enterprise. This puts him on a collision course with those logicians who seek to distinguish good from bad reasoning by a direct appeal to feeling (*gefühl*). For instance, the German logician Christoph von Sigwart, Peirce notes, "bases all logic upon our invincible mental repulsion against contradiction, or, as he calls it, 'the immediate feeling of necessity'" (CP2.209). This emotivist approach to logic, which at the time was particularly popular in Germany, is a form of psychologism—the view that logic should be grounded in a descriptive account of actual mental processes, such as the association of ideas, which ultimately falls under the purview of psychology. Peirce strongly objects to this on the ground that we sometimes feel perfectly confident about something only to discover much later that we were utterly wrong, and this type of theory gives us no tools for separating such cases from those where our confidence is justified.[3] Grounding logic in ethics and esthetics, and the latter two in phenomenology, is Peirce's response to psychologism in logic.[4]

Declaring logic a normative science puts the notion of self-control right at the center: It makes little sense to develop a theory of how people should reason if people have no control over how they do reason. Peirce further considers thinking an active affair. It is something we *do*, not something we passively undergo—as, say, a muscle spasm—even though sometimes, as with a sudden insight, our thoughts appear that way. Peirce consequently calls logic "the theory of deliberate thinking," adding that "to say that any thinking is deliberate is to imply that it is controlled with a view to making it conform to a purpose or ideal" (EP2:376). This raises several questions: What is this ideal? Does determining what the ideal is befall to logic, or does logic depend for this on a more basic science? And, are there multiple ideals, or is there in the end only one ultimate ideal? Now we may be tempted to say that the aim of thought is truth. But were we to do that, we would be running ahead of ourselves. For one thing, it would do little to answer our questions, as why would anyone aim for truth, what is this truth to begin with, and is it really the logician's task to determine what it is and whether it is worth striving after?

The realization that logic is the theory of deliberate thinking and that thinking is a form of action paves the way for grounding logic in ethics, where the latter is understood as "the theory of self-controlled, or deliberate, conduct" (CP1.191). Thus conceived, ethics is a broader science within which logic appears as a specialized subdiscipline. Briefly put, whereas ethics studies all self-controlled conduct, logic studies only that self-controlled conduct that aims at representing something.

As indicated, the science of ethics Peirce has in mind is a *theoretical* science, not a practical one. One would be clearly mistaken, says Peirce, to develop ethics in the practical sense without first gaining a solid understanding of psychology and logic, since they feature prominently in all moral deliberations of a practical kind. Peirce even goes so far as saying that given the current state of philosophy it is irresponsible, if not immoral, to apply philosophy to any real-life ethical problems. Though the study of theoretical ethics may make you a more moral person, Peirce doubts this is true, and he even suggests that the reverse is more likely. A theoretical treatise on ethics, he argues, is bound to have the same effect as Gaspard Coriolis's *Analytic Mechanics of the Game of Billiards* will have on your game of billiards—the deliberation it invites is much more likely to worsen your skills than to improve them (EP2:197). To distinguish his theoretical ethics from what usually goes under the name, Peirce suggests at one point using the term *antethics* (EP2:377).

This ethics, or antethics, is the discipline that seeks to relate our actions to certain ends that we believe are worth pursuing. It is "the theory of the conformity of action to an ideal" (EP2:377). This still raises the question of what those ideals are, whether it befalls to ethics to determine what they are, and whether there is one ultimate ideal or whether there are several. Peirce answers the second question negatively. Ethics asks essentially how we should direct our actions *given* certain preconceived ideals that we are willing to accept. Finding what is worth directing our actions to, Peirce considers an altogether different issue and one that requires a different mindset from the investigator. Peirce consequently makes it the object of a separate discipline, the science of ideals, which he identifies with esthetics. The aim of this science is to identify "that which is objectively admirable without any ulterior reason" (CP1.191). Given the discussion in the previous chapter, it is clear that esthetics as it is here conceived itself depends on the pre-normative science of phenomenology—the study of phenomena without *any* motive, not even that of determining what is admirable, and what is not.

Esthetics is typically defined as the science of sensuous beauty. In fact, Peirce defines it as such for the *Century Dictionary*.[5] This is not, however, what Peirce has in mind here. Taking an almost contrarian stance, he argues that the science of esthetics "has been handicapped by the definition of it as the theory of beauty" (CP2.199). The concept of beauty, he says, "is but the product of this science, and a very inadequate attempt it is to grasp what it is that esthetics seeks to make clear" (id.). Moreover, beauty is typically conceived as a quality of feeling, and Peirce refuses to accept that "any particular quality of feeling is admirable without a reason" without a "strenuous proof" for that (CP1.612). Instead, Peirce starts from the idea that the charge of esthetics is to discover what is admirable "without any reason for being admirable beyond its inherent character" (id.) and without preempting the discussion by stating that this is merely a particular quality of feeling.

Returning to the division of the sciences, we can say that the esthetician has at his disposal phenomenology and mathematics, but nothing else. This includes the doctrine of the categories developed in the previous chapter. Application of the latter leads Peirce to the following: "an object, to be esthetically good, must have a multitude of parts so related to one another as to impart *a positive simple immediate quality to their totality*; and whatever does this is, in so far, esthetically good, no matter what the particular quality of the total may be" (CP5.132; emphasis added). This would be so, Peirce continues, even if that quality "be such as to nauseate us, to scare us, or otherwise to disturb us to the point of throwing us out of the mood of esthetic enjoyment, out of the mood of simply contemplating the embodiment of the quality" (id.). The quality Peirce has in mind here is thus one that pertains to the *object* of our contemplation and not necessarily to our contemplation of the object. Put differently, though a positive simple immediate quality of totality could be a subjective feeling of pleasure, such a feeling, though perhaps a good indicator of an esthetic ideal, is an accidental rather than an essential element of it.

Feeling pleasure, Peirce argues, is not the only end we strive after. Traditionally two more classes of ends have been distinguished: ends that serve the objective purposes of society, and ends that serve the rationalization of the universe (CP1.590). According to Peirce, only the last can be truly ultimate, which leads him to identify the esthetic quality with "the total unanalyzable impression of a reasonableness that has expressed itself in a creation" (R310:12; also Section 9.5). As he puts it elsewhere, "the one thing whose admirableness is not due to an ulterior reason is Reason itself comprehended in all its fullness, so far as we can comprehend it" (CP4.615). Moreover, as will be clear from what is said, this is not something we bring to the table ourselves, but is something we encounter—it lights up, as it were, within the phaneron—and we are either receptive to it or we are not. In Chapter 9, when discussing Peirce's evolutionary cosmology, I will return to this when touching upon the connection between reason and instinct, and Peirce's notion of concrete reasonableness.

In line with the above, Peirce identifies esthetics as "the science of the adorably admirable" (R1334:40), taking admiration to be "a high degree of emotional approval of, or delight in, any object as being such or acting as it does regardless of any ulterior considerations of utility, interest, morality, or truth."[6] By calling the admiration adorable Peirce means to say that the admiration is like the wholly self-effacing worship of a God. To distinguish this science from how esthetics is generally conceived (as the theory of sensuous beauty), Peirce at one point introduces the term *axiagastics*, a term that combines the Greek *axia* (worth, value) with *agamai*, which expresses "how the common people in primitive times looked upon their leaders with passionate admiration and devotion" (id.).

In sum, for Peirce, the esthetic ideal is a positive simple immediate quality of totality, no matter how it relates to anything we may strive after or how we may feel about it, and he comes to identify this with the full expression of reasonableness in a creation. Once we have found our esthetic ideal, Peirce continues in Kantian fashion by stating that it elicits a categorical imperative, or an unconditional command of consciousness that pronounces for or against it (CP5.133). This then brings us to ethics, the aim of which is to study how this ideal can be implemented in action, and subsequently to logic, which studies how this ideal can be implemented in the particular action of representing something.

4.2 Instinct versus reason

"The object of reasoning," Peirce writes in *Popular Science Monthly*, "is to find out, from the consideration of what we already know, something else which we do not know" (W3:244). From this he concludes that, "reasoning is good if it be such as to give a true conclusion from true premises, and not otherwise" (id.). This causes him to hold that logic is a normative science, the aim of which is to distinguish good reasoning, or reasoning that preserves truth, from bad reasoning, or reasoning that leads to falsehood. Later, Peirce writes: "Reasoning is good if it be dominated by such a *habit* as generally to give a true conclusion from true premises" (CP2.11; emphasis added), making it the aim of logic to develop good reasoning habits. This approach to logic presupposes not only that we should reason such as to preserve truth but also that we often fail to do so, and that we have a choice in the matter. Were we to always reason correctly and unable to do otherwise, logic would be an explanatory theory at best, like a theory about the circulation of blood.

Traditionally, reason is considered what makes us human. Aristotle famously separated us from the beasts by calling us the rational animal, and in the Plato-inspired Christian tradition it is through our ability to reason that we partake in the divine. When it is said that God created man after His own image, we are not expected to think of feet, eyebrows, or armpits, but of our soul, which is taken to be the seat of reason. Descartes even went so far as to separate this soul, or mind, from the body by declaring that mind and body are separate substances that have nothing in common. The upshot of all of this is that reason was considered a divinely inspired noble faculty that constitutes the core of our identity; it was considered eternal and allotted equally to all normal human beings.

Peirce, who is writing after Darwin, has a different take on this. Instead of reason being instilled ready-made from on high, our ability to reason is a natural accomplishment that is grounded in our problem-solving activity and the problem-solving activity of countless generations that came before us—the latter extending all the way back to homo erectus and beyond. This has several implications for how Peirce understands reason. First, reason is not eternal or unchanging but develops over time (and is still developing). Second, since our ability to reason is a product of our interaction with—or our adaptation to—the universe, our capacity to reason is not a divine light that shines through us, but a reflection of the order of the universe. Put differently, the universe is itself reasonable and our faculty of reasoning is a reflection of that. Third, since reasoning is grounded in our practical dealings with the world, it is not clear how well it fares when we apply it to subjects that are far removed from this, say when we reason about subatomic particles, multiple galaxies, God's omniscience, or infinite numbers.

Peirce's naturalistic account of reason also affects how he sees the relation between reason and instinct. Whereas traditionally reason was considered superior to instinct, Peirce takes the opposite view. Like reason, instinct is a product of the individual's interaction with the environment and a reflection of the reasonableness of the universe (Section 9.5). He further holds that instinct is subtler and less error prone than reason. In fact, reason's sole advantage to instinct, Peirce observes, is that it is reflective—"there is reasoning that reason itself condemns" (R832:2)—and the distinction between good and bad reasoning lies precisely therein. Instincts can fail, as when a turtle retracts in his shell when a car approaches, but instincts cannot correct themselves. In line with this, Peirce defines reasoning in Baldwin's *Dictionary* as "a process in which the reasoner is conscious that a judgment, the conclusion, is determined by other judgment or judgments, the premises, according to a general habit of thought, which he may not be able precisely to formulate, but which he approves as conducive to true knowledge" (2:426). The totality of these habits, which are directive, subject to self-control, and approved by the reasoner, constitutes a rudimentary science of logic which Peirce, following the medievals, calls our *logica utens* (HPPLS2:891). This *logica utens* is a rather haphazardly formed but seasoned grab bag of modes of inference. This opens up the possibility of—and even the need for—a systematic study of this *logica utens*. Still following the medievals, Peirce names the latter *logica docens*. Peirce is careful to add, though, that it would be a mistake to think that the motive behind this is to replace *logica utens* with a *logica docens*. Instead we should hold on to our instinctive ways of reasoning, especially in practical affairs. *Logica docens* is useful only "to compare theory with practice," or for some "peculiar and quite theoretical purpose" (NEM4:187).

Though Peirce places great weight on the need of studying logic, he rejects the traditional belief that we are driven primarily by reason rather than instinct. This traditional belief he thinks is an illusion caused by the circumstance that while we are typically unaware of our instincts, our reasoning plays out prominently in our consciousness (R410:1f).

That reason grows and has practical roots deeply affects how Peirce sees logic. All the important advances in logic are the (generalized) products of significant advances in actual problem solving—of actual cases of removing doubt. Solving a problem typically comes with the belief that similar cases can (and even should) be solved the same way. This, in turn, leads to a rule, or habit, however inchoate, that becomes part of our *logica utens*. Some of these rules will be unique to the individual, but most of them will not. In short, reason has its own fallible, contingent history. Especially during the modern age this history is predominantly the history of science. As Peirce observes in "The Fixation of Belief": "every work of science great enough to be remembered for a few generations affords some exemplification of the defective state of the art of reasoning of the time when it was written; and each chief step in science has been a lesson in logic" (W3:243). This is also why Peirce calls Antoine Lavoisier's alembics and cucurbits literally instruments of thought (id.). It is a mistake, he explains elsewhere, to take our reasoning "in that narrow sense in which silence and darkness are favorable to thought. It should rather be understood as covering all rational life, so that an experiment shall be *an operation of thought*" (CP2.420; emphasis added). In an essential way this brings thought out in the open. I return to this when discussing Peirce's philosophy of science (Chapter 6) and his conception of mind (Section 9.4). In the next section, we take a closer look at this *logica docens*.

4.3 The elementary modes of reasoning

As shown in the previous section, logic, or *logica docens*, concerns the systematic study of our *logica utens*. For Peirce, its main purpose is to draw up a natural classification of the arguments that constitute our *logical utens* and to examine their interrelations. In this sense, logic is not essentially different from biology, with its classification of species, or from chemistry, with its classification of elements. In the process, good arguments are separated from bad ones, and for the good ones their relative strength is ascertained. Following Locke and Kant, Peirce calls this part of logic *critic*.

Critic, however, is not the most basic part of logic. It is preceded by what Peirce calls *speculative grammar,* which considers a whole range of questions that should be dealt with before one begins classifying arguments. In this context "speculative," from the Latin *speculari* (to examine or observe) means theoretical as opposed to practical. Put generally, speculative grammar studies what must be true of a sign so it can convey meaning; that is to say, it is "the general theory of the nature and meanings of signs" (CP1.191).

Besides speculative grammar and critic, Peirce also distinguishes what he calls *speculative rhetoric,* or *methodeutic.* This third and highest branch of logic studies the "general conditions under which a problem presents itself for solution" (CP3.430). Traditionally, rhetoric refers to the art of persuasion. Peirce gives a different twist to this by declaring speculative rhetoric the art of discovery. In a sense, Peirce here reflects the view that it is the facts and not the opinions of others that should do the persuading. Moreover, as Peirce considers inquiry a decidedly communal affair—up to the point of making "solitary scientist" an oxymoron—speculative rhetoric does involve the art of communication and the art of persuasion also in the more traditional sense. Speculative rhetoric includes pragmatism, the theory of the economy of research, synechism (the view that whenever possible we should regard all things continuous), and what today we call philosophy of science.

Each of the three branches of logic depends on those that precede it. Peirce sometimes identifies speculative grammar with semeiotics, while at other times suggesting that semeiotics comprises all of logic. I return to semeiotics in the next chapter.

Before discussing Peirce's classification of arguments, let's first have a brief look at what an argument is. Peirce defines reasoning as the deliberate adoption of a belief (or proposition), called the conclusion, in consequence of the admitted truth of another belief (or proposition). The latter is called the premise. For one to be justified in claiming that the conclusion is true—either necessarily or with some degree of probability—both the premise (or premises) and what Peirce calls the leading principle must be true. The leading principle can be strictly defined as "whatever is considered requisite besides the premises to determine the necessary or probable truth of the conclusion" (W2:24). Typically such leading principles are furnished by our *logica utens*. Say we derive the new belief that Socrates died from our existing belief that he was a man. The justification of this lies in the belief that Socrates was a man and the unexpressed leading principle that all men die. When we subject the inference "Socrates was a man, hence Socrates died" to logical criticism we make this leading principle explicit by adding it as a premise, which gives us the following:

Socrates was a man,
All men die;
Socrates died.

Now, it is also a leading principle of our *logica utens* that if a leading principle justifies drawing a conclusion in one situation, that same principle can be used when the situation is sufficiently similar. In this way, a successful leading principle comes to manifest itself as a habit of reasoning; that is, as a habit that determines an inference. For instance, whenever we hear that someone is a man, we habitually conclude that he will die unless he has died already. On this view, it is not the subjective feeling, or *Gefühl*, of the reasoner that signals the validity of the argument, but the objective consideration of the applicability of a leading principle. The acceptance of a certain leading principle relates to the purpose behind the argument, so that it comes to act like a norm or prescription. We reason deliberately when we make a conscious decision what leading principle to apply.

Based on the above, we can say that someone who reasons well is someone who has developed good habits of reasoning—meaning that his reasoning is governed by leading principles that are true. It is not requisite, however, that he has a clear apprehension of these habits or principles—in fact, one's notion of certain principles may be so vague that when first seeing them explicitly stated one might even reject them. For instance, for the fundamentalist Christian the principle that all men die conflicts with another established principle, namely that the bible is never wrong. It conflicts, because Enoch was a man who did not die, and so was Elijah. (Instead of dying both went straight to heaven.)

In our classification of arguments, we must first distinguish between those habits of reasoning, or leading principles, that are good (or true), and those that are not. As Peirce puts it, "To say that an argumentation is valid is to say that it is *as truthful as it pretends to be*. It is essential to reasoning . . . that it should be accompanied by the reflection that it belongs to a class of reasonings, few or none of which lead from truth to falsity. All reasoning, therefore, makes a pretension; and if that pretension is true, the reasoning is valid" (CP2.446, emphasis added). Hence, the argument of affirming the consequent (if p then q, q; hence, p) is not valid, because it *pretends* to be more truthful than it is. Its purported validity derives from its semblance to a deductive inference—one that "pretends to be such that it is logically impossible for the premises to be true while the conclusion is false" (CP2.447), whereas its real truthfulness is at best covertly abductive or inductive. This is why we call it a fallacy rather than a mistake.

Peirce further distinguishes leading principles that complete an argument—such as "All men die" or "the bible never errs"—from those that govern an argument that is already complete. The former he calls *material* leading principles, the latter he calls *logical* leading principles (Baldwin, 2:1). Because a logical leading principle is one that governs a complete argument, it can contain "no *fact* not implied or observable in the premises," as otherwise the argument was not complete (CP3.166, emphasis added). Such principles are, as Peirce puts it, "merely rules for the illative transformation of the symbols of the particular system employed," and he adds that if we are to change the system, those rules may change considerably as well (CP2.599). With the notion of a logical leading principle we are entering the realm of mathematics. In mathematics, we can create models, or systems, to represent illative transformation—the move we make when using words such as "hence," "ergo," or "therefore" and by which we transform one string of symbols (the premises) into another (the conclusion). The notion of material implication in Russell and Whitehead's *Principa Mathematica* is an example of this. In short, given a system of illative transformation, a complete argument is one that is structured such that, if the premises are taken to be true, the conclusion cannot be said to be false without violating the system's rules.

However, logic as Peirce conceives it, is not a part of mathematics, but is a positive science. It is about the real world we experience. Peirce further believes that, as such it is inspired by the general presupposition, or the *faith,* that the positive facts we are reasoning about allow our reasoning to carry our beliefs in the long run "toward certain predestinate conclusions which are the same for all men" (CP3.161); these conclusions are predestinate in the sense that our reasoning about them does not alter them—they are, to put it loosely "set in advance" and in the process of reasoning we "discover" them. I will return to this assumption more into detail in Chapter 6. For now it suffices to say that if a leading principle is of a type that tends to bring us toward a predestinate conclusion that is shared by all, it is true, otherwise it is not.

Let us now return to the issue of the classification of arguments. Taking his cues from the medieval doctrine of *consequentiae*, Peirce distinguishes three irreducible classes of arguments—where *class* is understood extensionally as "the total of whatever objects there may be ... which are of a certain description" (CP1.204)—and he calls them deduction, induction, and abduction (for the last he also employs the terms hypothesis and retroduction). As late as 1911, Peirce writes that these three classes constitute "three absolutely disparate ways of reasoning" and that there are "very strong *probable* reasons for believing there is no fourth" (NEM3:177f).

In Peirce's early work, the three classes of reasoning surface as three ways in which a rule, a case, and a result can be combined, as the following example shows:

deduction
All the beans in this bag are white (Rule),
These beans are from this bag (Case);
These beans are white (Result).

induction
These beans are white (Result),
These beans are from this bag (Case);
All the beans in this bag are white (Rule).

abduction
All the beans in this bag are white (Rule),
These beans are white (Result);
These beans are from this bag (Case).

As it turns out, however, the picture quickly gets much more complicated. And as Peirce comes to realize, this formal way of defining the three modes of inference fails to bring out the real nature of induction and abduction. In what follows I give an impressionistic sketch of this more complicated picture, discussing first deduction, then induction, and finally abduction.

4.4 Deduction and induction

In the *Century Dictionary,* Peirce defines *deduction* as: "derivation as a result of assumed principles or hypotheses; necessary inference," and he defines the verb *to deduce* as "to derive or conclude as a result of [an assumed] principle; draw as a necessary conclusion" (CD:1495).[7] Similarly, Peirce defines deduction in Baldwin's *Dictionary* as any inference where "the facts presented in the premises could not under any imaginable circumstances be true without involving the truth of the conclusion, which is therefore accepted with necessary modality," and he adds that "it is to ideal states of things alone—or to real states of things as ideally conceived, always more or less departing from the reality—that deduction applies" (2:428).

With its reference to necessity and to assumed principles or hypotheses, the above is in essence a definition of the mathematical reasoning that was discussed in Section 2.3. As we saw there also, deduction can come in many forms, and includes besides corollarial deduction (which is favored by authors of logic textbooks) also theorematic deduction. Peirce includes among deduction all necessary reasoning, including what is called mathematical induction[8] and "those probable reasonings which predict results as true in the long run, but excluding those inferences which are regarded as being open to correction in the long run" (CD:1495). I return to Peirce's conception of the long run in Chapter 6. Because Peirce is a thoroughgoing fallibilist, holding that we can never be absolutely certain about anything, we can never say with certainty that an argument is deductive. Even the simplest deduction may prove to be wrong in the future. Later, Peirce defines deduction in terms of compulsive, rather than necessary reasoning. "Deduction," he writes, "first points to the premises and their relation, and then shakes its fist in your face and tells you 'Now, by God, you've *got to* admit the conclusion'" (R754:3). This compulsion is an instance of degenerate secondness (Section 3.2). According to Peirce, one of the great defects of logic is that logicians have largely limited themselves to deduction only, and they further restricted themselves only to syllogisms. By thus making corollarial deduction the paradigm of logic, logicians have science little or nothing to offer.

In the *Century Dictionary* Peirce defines *induction* as "the process of drawing a general conclusion from particular cases; the inference from the character of a sample to that of the whole lot sampled" (CD:3068). And as he puts it elsewhere: "Induction is that kind of reasoning which from what is true of a part, concludes what is true of the whole."[9] The classic example is that of a bag of beans. If two-thirds of the beans drawn from the bag are white, the conclusion that two-thirds of the beans remaining in the bag are white too seems warranted, and the mechanism through which we arrive at this conclusion is likely to become part of our *logica utens*. The argument clearly lacks the force—or the compulsion—of a deductive argument, as drawing a few handful of beans from a bag, and seeing that two-thirds of them is white, still leaves open the possibility, say, that less than half of the beans in the bag are white. The example also shows that inductive arguments can be of various strengths. It makes significant difference whether you base your conclusion on taking only three beans from the bag and seeing that two-thirds of them are white, and taking half the beans out of the bag and drawing the same conclusion.

That induction lacks the force of deduction is for Peirce no reason to omit it from logic proper. Quite the contrary, given that the aim of logic is to tell us how we should reason when we want to preserve truth, it befalls on the logician to determine what makes inductions strong, and how to avoid weak inductions. In fact, Peirce spends considerable time and effort developing a theory of induction and debunking poor inductive arguments, the latter ranging from his criticism of *Phantasms of the Living*—a work that purportedly showed that we could talk with the dead—to detailed analyses of error-reduction strategies in geodesy.

What, in Peirce's view, justifies induction as a rational mode of inference is that, as far as we can tell, it is the best way of making conjectures about what we do not know. In addition, there is good (inductive) reason to believe that induction is self-correcting. As Peirce writes in the *Century Dictionary*: "Its character is that, though the special conclusion drawn might not be verified in the long run, yet similar conclusions would be, and in the long run the premises would be so corrected as to change the conclusion and make it correct" (CD:3068). Note that this is a methodological justification of induction, not a metaphysical one. As far as the latter is concerned, Peirce repeatedly denies the at-the-time-popular view that induction is justified by the uniformity in nature, implying that the future resembles the past.

In brief, when we reason inductively we let what we know (e.g. the composition of the beans taken from the bag) determine what we do not know (the composition of the beans remaining in the bag), and let the experience we gain in the process correct false beliefs and refine our methods. This means that in induction too there is some sort of compulsion at work, albeit that here it is not an internal compulsion—the mind itself setting us straight by showing that we cannot think things otherwise without creating some irreconcilable incompatibility among our beliefs—but an external one. Like deduction, however, induction cannot *originate* any idea; it can only tell us "approximately how often, in the course of such experience as our experiments go towards constituting, a given sort of event occurs" (Baldwin 2:426f). For Peirce, the true source of originality lies in the third type of reasoning, which he calls *abduction* though he also uses the terms *retroduction, presumption,* and *hypothesis.*

4.5 Abduction

The *Century Dictionary* contains no entry for abduction (or retroduction) as a mode of inference.[10] However, Peirce defines the term as follows in Baldwin's *Dictionary*:

> Upon finding himself confronted with a phenomenon unlike what he would have expected under the circumstances, he looks over its features and notices some remarkable character or relation among them, which he at once recognizes as being characteristic of some conception with which the mind is already stored, so that a theory is suggested which would *explain* (this is, render necessary) that which is surprising in the phenomena. (2:427)

A classic example is Johannes Kepler's discovery of the orbit of Mars. Kepler had Tycho Brahe's observations to work with. Brahe had proved himself a truly outstanding observer who possessed the added talent to precisely measure and calculate the positions of the stars and the planets he observed. The result was an enormous mass of new data. For Peirce, Kepler's conclusion that Mars revolves in an ellipse with the sun as one of its foci, was clearly the result of an argument, and an argument that is neither deductive nor inductive. Kepler's argument involved: accepting the Copernican heliocentric view (which Brahe did not), realizing that the sun's size may have something to do with the movements of the planets, and finding that descriptions of the motion of Mars are simpler when the sun is made a fixed point of reference. Kepler's theory still only approximated Brahe's data, which required further modifications that eventually caused Kepler to conclude that the orbit of Mars is not a perfect circle but that there must be a slight compression of the orbit. This made Kepler conjecture that the true orbit of Mars is an ellipse. This final move, which meant rejecting the long-held belief in the circular orbits of heavenly bodies, only came about after other plausible hypotheses—that space is not homogenous, that some of Brahe's observations must have been flawed, that Kepler's own calculations contained mistakes—had been entertained and rejected.

In its most general form this type of inference can be captured as follows:

> Some surprising fact B is observed,
> If A were true, B would be explicable as a matter of course;
> Hence, there is reason to suspect that A is true.

Thus, when trying to develop the orbit of Mars for the new Copernican system while holding on to the common preconception that heavenly bodies move in perfect circles, Kepler began with the observation that there are slight eccentricities in the orbit of Mars (surprising fact B). Next he looked for possible causes that would explain these eccentricities. This led him to a hypothetical cause (suspected fact A), which subsequent research either denied or confirmed. If the former, it caused him to look for alternatives to suspected fact A that could also explain surprising fact B.

Now, how do we find these alternatives? For Peirce it comes down in the end to educated guesses. This causes some to argue that abduction is not really a mode of inference. However, something more can be said about these guesses: they typically must take into account as many of the relevant facts as possible; our past experience and other beliefs make some of them more likely than others; each alternative comes with its own presuppositions and implications; some alternatives are far easier to confirm or deny than others; and so on. Thus, in Kepler's case, the first guess he should consider is that there are mistakes in the calculations: it's not unlikely, it's least invasive in terms of requiring modifications to existing theory or having to dismiss past observations, and it's relatively easy to check. If no mistakes are found, as happened in Kepler's case, considerations like the ones listed above, which are largely considerations from the economy of research, will suggest where we should look next.

The procedure of educated guessing outlined above shows that in abduction, as in deduction and induction, we consciously proceed according to some general habit, or method, which is such that it tends to lead us to rational explanations, and hence to the truth, which, as we will see in Chapter 8, is nothing but a rational explanation that is beyond all possible doubt. Hence, even though abduction "is very little hampered by logical rules" (CP5.188), and lacks the self-correctiveness of induction, it should still be considered a mode of logical inference, and as we will see in Chapter 7, Peirce explicitly identifies pragmatism as the logic of abduction. The above procedure also shows that abduction is only possible to the extent that we are able to extract from the countless alternatives that are logically possible, those that are fruitful. I return to this in Section 9.5.

In contemporary literature, abduction is sometimes referred to as "inference to the best explanation."[11] This phrase is not used by Peirce and is best avoided because there are several problems with it. Most importantly, this phrase is suited not only for abduction, but also, and perhaps even more so, for induction. The conclusion that two-thirds of the beans in the bag is white is quite clearly the "best explanation" for the fact that two-thirds of the beans in the sample drawn from the bag is white. Abduction generally does not draw conclusions with that kind of strength. Nor does it contain any mechanism for determining whether a successful explanation is indeed the best one. The most we can say is that it is a *plausible* explanation (or explanatory hypothesis) or the one that for some reason we find the most plausible.

What justifies abduction as a mode of inference is that we really have no choice. When we refuse to engage in it—which we can, as reasoning is a form of self-controlled, hence voluntary, conduct—our only option is to remain, as Peirce puts it "without any hope of learning the truth" (R440:35). Regarding the ultimate justification of both abduction and induction, Peirce maintains that "the only *rationale* of those methods is essentially deductive or necessary," meaning that the closer they come to the ideal of necessary reasoning—arguments where the conclusion cannot possibly be false if the premises are true—the more justified we are in using them.

The three types of reasoning outlined above are ideal types, and Peirce considers them the three most basic types of reasoning. Typically, our reasoning involves combinations of them. A particularly powerful combination—one that is characteristic of much scientific reasoning—combines abduction first with deduction and then with induction.

What sets the train of reasoning in motion, Peirce argues, is some surprising phenomenon that sufficiently compels us to look for an explanation. Though this means that every discovery is in the end an accident, Peirce is keenly aware that people can train themselves to be struck by minutiae to which most of us are blind. In that sense, Peirce argues, discovery is not an accident.

We first try to extract from the surprising phenomenon and the beliefs we already have plausible hypotheses that would account for it. Next we develop a strategy for testing these hypotheses. Here the driving force is the economy of research. Empirical tests can be very costly, especially when expensive equipment is required, or when obtaining a sufficiently representative sample demands a considerable investment of time and energy. Once a hypothesis is decided upon, the next step is to bring in the mathematician. Recall that the mathematician is not at all concerned whether the hypothesis is true, but merely seeks to determine what follows from it necessarily. The aim is to draw out testable (experiential, or practical) consequences that could show the hypothesis true or false. The third and last step is that of induction. Here one returns to the phenomena to study whether these derived consequences agree with our experience. When this is an inference from instances that are not discrete and countable, Peirce calls it *qualitative induction*; when it involves discrete and countable instances—like beans drawn from a bag—he calls it *quantitative induction*; and when it is based on experience broadly conceived—as when we say that because the earth has always turned around its axis every 24 hours, it will do so tomorrow—he calls it *crude induction*.[12] In short, abduction furnishes us with explanatory hypotheses, or theories, deduction draws out their logical implications, and induction verifies (or falsifies) these implications, and by doing so verifies (or falsifies) the hypothesis.

4.6 The logic of relatives

Traditionally, logicians have restricted their studies to subject-predicate logic. This is in part because they presupposed a substance-attribute metaphysics on which there exist only individual things with properties. For Peirce, this is not only restrictive, but also misleading. Traditional logic wrongly suggests that each inference has but a single conclusion that can be reached through the rote application of rigid rules—something even a machine can do. The logic of relatives shows, Peirce argues, that from any proposition one can deduce "an endless series of necessary consequences," and that "a number of distinct lines of inference may be taken, none leading to another," and he cites the theory of numbers as a case in point (Baldwin 2:449). Peirce thereby rejects Kant's view that deductive logic is analytic. Deduction involves much more than making explicit what is already contained in the premises: "matter entirely foreign to the premises may appear in the conclusion" (id.). The logic of relatives also underscores that deduction involves observation and experimentation upon diagrams.

The logic of relatives, or the logic of relations, differs from ordinary subject-predicate logic in that it considers propositions that have multiple subject-nouns, as in "Romeo gives a flower to Juliette." A relative, as Peirce defines it, is the incomplete proposition in which the subject-nouns are replaced by blanks, as in, "____ gives ____ to ____." This can be represented algebraically as g_{ijk} (where i represents Romeo, j a flower, and k Juliette), or geometrically as:

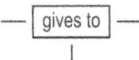

FIGURE 4.1 *Graphical representation of "__ gives __ to __."*

A logic of relations implies that in addition to individuals and their properties there are also relations. Peirce's conception of hypostatic abstraction and *entia rationis* discussed in Section 2.3 even enables us to conceive of the relation without the relata. Peirce's view further allows that these relations are more than mere *entia rationis*. They may be *entia realis* as well—that is, they can be real.

When discussing the categories in Section 3.2, I introduced a mathematical model to identify the indecomposable elements of the phaneron. This model can be used to show that a triadic relation cannot be reduced to a set of dyadic relations, and that all polyadic relations can be reduced to combinations of triads. The same is true for relatives. Relatives also cannot be reduced to a combination of dyads. "Romeo gives a flower to Juliette" clearly expresses more than the mere conjunction of "Romeo gave a flower" and "Juliette got one." However, all relatives with more than three blanks can be reduced to combinations of triadic relatives.

One way to prove this is with the method of forking trees. A dyadic proposition, like "John is tall," can be represented as follows,

FIGURE 4.2 *Graphic representation of a dyadic relative.*

(For the argument behind this, see Section 3.2.) Similarly, the triadic "Romeo gives a flower to Juliette," can be represented as,

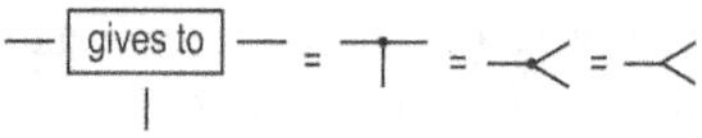

FIGURE 4.3 *Graphic representation of a triadic relative.*

Now when we use these two figures to create more complicated diagrams, we find that no matter how many dyadic figures we combine, the result will always be a dyadic figure. No combination of dyadic relations can ever give us a triadic one:

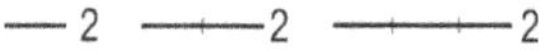

FIGURE 4.4 *Adding dyads to dyads only gives dyads.*

We also find that we can form any polyadic figure from triadic figures, so that any polyadic relative can be construed as a combination of triadic relatives, for example:

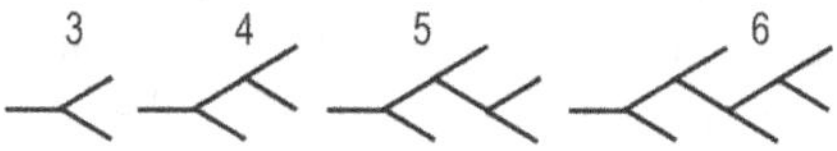

FIGURE 4.5 *With triads we can construe any polyad.*

Hence, though we need a separate logic for triadic relatives, once we have that we do not also need separate logics for higher order relatives, as they can always be expressed in terms of triadic relatives.

4.7 The geometry of thought: Existential graphs

Peirce was very active in mathematical logic. We find in his work the origin of modern quantification theory (the terms "quantification" and "quantifier" are his), an early form of truth-functional analysis (including truth tables), significant contributions to the logic of induction and probability theory, and a developed algebra for relations (or logic of relatives). Peirce also developed a semantic for three-valued logic a decade before Emil Post's dissertation (which is usually cited as the origin of three-valued logic), he developed a single-connective logic more than three decades before Henry Sheffer introduced the famous stroke now named after him, and he discovered what is now known as Peirce's law: $((P \to Q) \to P) \to P$ (P must be true if there is a proposition Q such that the truth of P follows from the truth of "if P then Q"). In 1922, the well-known Polish logician Jan Łukasiewicz identified Gottlob Frege, Charles Peirce, and Bertrand Russell as the three most prominent representatives of mathematical logic.[13] More than half a century later, W. V. O. Quine similarly remarked that for him modern logic begins with Peirce and Frege,[14] and he considers Peirce's 1870 "Description of a Notation for the Logic of Relatives" (W2:359–430) a precursor to Russell and Whitehead's *Principia Mathemathica*.[15] More systematically, we can say that Peirce draws together the old Aristotelian logic of terms, George Boole's calculus of classes, and Augustus De Morgan's logic of relations in a manner that proved most productive.

Although a discussion of Peirce's work in mathematical logic lies well beyond the scope of this volume, I want to briefly touch upon his existential graphs, as it brings together several of the points discussed so far. Though Peirce has been working with graphs before, the idea of developing a full-fledged logic from them comes to him only in 1896.[16] Over a decade later he calls the existential graphs that came out of this his *chef d'oeuvre*.[17]

Earlier we saw that deduction not only requires the observation of relationships, but often also requires us to experiment, that is, perform certain acts and observe the results (Section 2.3). As we saw, much comes down to devising some sort of diagram that is at once representative of the situation and conducive to experimentation.

Using this approach we were able to conclude, in Chapter 2, that the angles of a triangle equal two right angles. Although algebraic relations are also diagrammatic, they are not iconic. That is to say, they do not *resemble,* or depict, the relationships they represent. Instead their applicability is determined by rules that are set a priori. For Peirce this is an important strike against algebraic systems. Remaining closer to how we operate when we are engaged in the activity we call reasoning, Peirce sees the graphs as a superior method, especially when our aim is "to facilitate the anatomy, and thereby the physiology of deductive reasonings" (R500:11).

In Chapter 2, we also learned that the idea of mathematics as the science of counting and measuring is no longer tenable. The result is a thorough restructuring of the discipline. When considering mathematics as a science of discovery, Peirce argues, we can divide geometry, or the study of space, into topology, projective geometry, and metrics. *Topology* is the most basic of the three. It is subject only to a single law: only such transformations are allowed that leave the *connection* of the parts unaffected. As Peirce puts it: "objects can be made to expand, to contract, to bend, to twist, and in short to move free from any law, excepting only that it is nowhere to be broken or welded" (PM:122). For this reason, topology is sometimes called rubber sheet geometry. Given how Peirce defines mathematics (Section 2.2), it will not come as a surprise that Peirce even allows this rule to be broken, albeit only if "the violation be specifically supposed to take place on a definite occasion and by a defined motion" (id.). *Projective geometry* (also called graphics or geometrical optic) is in effect an extension of the doctrine of linear perspective; it is a geometry of straight lines. Now we cannot in any meaningful way single out or define a straight line within topology. Instead, the straight line is the product of an externally imposed restriction. As Peirce sees it, the concept of a straight line derives from the *physical* notion of a ray of light, which can be geometrically defined as the unobstructed movement of a single particle. Hence, the identification of a straight line and the rules that govern it are extraneous to topology itself. Or, to put it differently, projective geometry can be said to presuppose topology while imposing certain restrictions upon it. *Metrics*, finally, is the science of spatial quantities. For this, we have to again introduce a new concept. This time it is the idea of a rigid body. It is by the (multiple) displacements of this body that we can express other bodies in terms of it, as when we take a one-inch ruler to measure the length of a desk. Again, the restrictions imposed upon this rigid body, and the rules that guide its displacements, are extraneous both to topology and projective geometry. Hence, metrics presupposes projective geometry while imposing its own set of restrictions upon it. The old geometry was pretty much confined to metrics. Returning to the graphs we can say that when developing the graphs Peirce aims to ground them directly into topology, so that the most basic system of graphs requires besides its own stipulations only what is required by topology, which as we saw is hardly anything at all.

Peirce develops three systems of graphs: the alpha, beta, and gamma graphs. The *alpha graphs* are the most basic of the three. They form a geometrical rendition of the propositional calculus. As they are intended to depict only relations between whole propositions, the alpha graphs only treat of sentential connectives, such as "and," "or," and "not." The *beta graphs* cover predicate logic. They deal not only with sentential connectives, but also with the internal structure of propositions: subjects and predicates, and quantification. Thus, the beta graphs can express the logic of relatives. The *gamma graphs* are distinguished from the first two in that they can also take into account abstractions. In this way, we can subject the graphs themselves to a graphical analysis and thus use them to "reflect or turn round upon thought itself and make it the object of thought" (R450:28). For that reason, Peirce also calls the gamma graphs second intentional graphs (CP4.469). Peirce moreover sought to use the gamma graphs to express modality.[18]

In this triad, the beta graphs presuppose and build upon the alpha graphs, whereas the gamma graphs presuppose and build upon the beta graphs. Of the three, the gamma graphs are least developed. Though the alpha, beta, and gamma graphs only deal with necessary reasoning, or deduction, Peirce believed that graphs could be used also to represent induction and abduction (R296:8).

Let us briefly look at the graphs to get a better idea of what Peirce's graphical logic looks like. The first element is the paper on which the graphs are drawn. Peirce calls this the *sheet of assertion*. An *assertion* is made whenever someone claims something is true. Consequently, any assertion written on the sheet of assertion is claimed to be true.[19] For convenience we abbreviate assertions with capital letters. Since all assertions on the sheet of assertion are claimed to be true, we can only *deny* an assertion by removing it from the sheet of assertion. This we do by quite literally cutting it out, a process that can be visualized by drawing a closed line around the letter. If we adhere to material implication—where "if P then Q" is taken to be logically equivalent with "not (P and not-Q)"—all common logical operators can be easily expressed in graphs (Figure 4.6). This allows us to build a functionally complete propositional logic in any medium that is sufficiently static (paper, computer, imagination) using only variables and cuts.

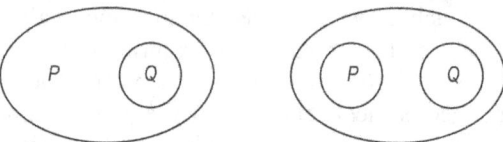

FIGURE 4.6 *Existential Graphs. The left figure represents material implication; the right figure disjunction. Both combined represent* (P→Q) & (P v Q).

Since we want the graphs to represent the analysis of arguments, we must find a way to have them show whether a certain conclusion flows from a certain set of assertions (or premises). This we can do by writing, or drawing, the assertions on one sheet of paper and the conclusion on another. Having done so we must next try to transform the first graph into the second while allowing only such transformations that are truth preserving. This procedure is not any different from how in Chapter 2 we used Euclid's rules for transforming geometrical figures to show that the angles of a triangle equal two right angles. This, then, raises the question whether we can develop a complete set of transformation rules that can show us whether a conclusion necessarily follows from a set of assertions, no matter how complicated the assertions or the conclusions are.[20]

CHAPTER FIVE

Semeiotics, or the doctrine of signs

In the final chapter of his *Essay Concerning Human Understanding* (1690), John Locke divides science into: *physics*, which studies "The Nature of Things, as they are in themselves, and their Relations, and their manner of Operations"; *practics*, which concerns "the Skill of Right applying our own Powers and Actions, for the Attainment of Things good and useful"; and *semeiotics*.[1] This last term he derives from the Greek *semeion*, for "sign" or "signal." According to Locke, it is the business of semeiotics—which like Peirce he also calls the doctrine of signs, and which like Peirce he also identifies with logic—"to consider the Nature of Signs, the Mind makes use of for the Understanding of Things, or conveying its Knowledge to others."[2] When Locke writes these words the term was commonly used in medicine. For instance, James Hart, in his 1625 *Anatomy of Urine*, calls semeiotics the art that teaches us the nature, causes, and substance of a disease by its signs. Locke introduces the term into philosophy, pretty much retaining its meaning while significantly extending its reference. In essence, Locke proposes to apply the method developed for interpreting the symptoms of diseases to all knowledge, and his *Essay*, particularly Book 4, is an attempt to do this. There is a clear Lockean influence on Whatley's *Logic*, the book that so much enchants Peirce as a child (Section 1.1), and on George Boole, whose mathematical logic deeply influences the early Peirce. In the second chapter of his *Laws of Thought*, Boole uses a rudimentary doctrine of signs to explicate and legitimate his approach to logic, writing that: "in studying the laws of signs, we are in effect studying the manifested laws of reasoning."[3] On the relation between logic and semeiotics Peirce's views shift over time. At first he sees it as covering only part of logic, especially speculative grammar, but in the end he takes it, as Locke does, as covering all logic.

In the previous chapter, we saw that Peirce divided logic into speculative grammar, critic, and speculative rhetoric. With this division in mind we can give the following brief summary of logic conceived as semeiotics: speculative grammar studies "the essential nature of the different kinds of signs," critic studies "the general conditions of their relations to their objects," and speculative rhetoric studies "the general conditions of their fulfilling their purposes."[4] Earlier Peirce similarly distinguishes "three ways in which signs can be studied": speculative grammar studies "the general conditions of their having any meaning," logic "the conditions of their truth," and speculative rhetoric "the conditions of their transferring their meaning to other signs" (R439:2). In the twentieth century, Charles Morris introduces this threefold division into mainstream philosophy under the headings of semantics, syntax, and pragmatics.

Of course, if semeiotics embodies Peirce's new approach to logic, then, given that Peirce considers logic a normative science, semeiotics—insofar as its object is subject to self-control—is a normative science also, whether it concerns the development of a sign vocabulary (speculative grammar), the study of the control of signs in relation to their object (critic), or of their interpretation (speculative rhetoric).

Over the years, Peirce gives various descriptions of semeiotics. He calls it the study of "the necessary conditions to which signs must conform in order to fulfill their functions as signs" (R693:101), "the general theory of signs of all kinds, not merely in relation to their objects but in every way" (R1334:43), and "the general physiology of signs" (R641:2).[5]

Peirce leaves semeiotics in a clearly unfinished state. In 1907, he writes that he sees himself as "a pioneer, or rather a backwoodsman, in the work of clearing and opening up ... semiotic," adding that "the field [is] too vast, the labor too great, for a first-comer" (EP2:413). From the perspective of Peirce's natural classification of the sciences, the study of semeiotics has to be taken up by some group of investigators. In Peirce's view this task quite naturally befalls to logicians (understood in the traditional sense where logic is largely confined to critic). One rather trivial issue on which emotions run high is the proper spelling of the word. In Peirce we find four different variants: semeiotic, semeotic, semiotic, and semeiotics. Interestingly, semiotics, which is the variant most commonly used today, is not used by Peirce. For reasons not altogether arbitrary I choose semeiotics.

In the current chapter, I present a brief overview of Peirce's semeiotics, and say something about how it connects with the topics of subsequent chapters, such as Peirce's pragmatism, his theory of inquiry, his philosophy of mind, and his cosmology. After a brief history of semeiotics, I will discuss Peirce's definition of the sign and the conceptions of object and interpretant it entails. Next follows an analysis that culminates in a classification, or better perhaps a typology, of signs.

5.1 Two schools of semeiotics

Contemporary semeiotics divides roughly into two schools, one of which finds its origin in Peirce, the other in the Swiss Linguist Ferdinand de Saussure. The latter, which comes to dominate in the twentieth century, is originally called semiology, but of late "semiotics" has been taking over as the label of choice. Though Peirce and Saussure develop their views independently, the Saussurean approach should be discussed briefly, as this has been the dominant tradition in the twentieth century. Saussure develops his semeiotics in his *Course of General Linguistics,* which appeared posthumously in 1916.

Being a linguist, Saussure develops his semeiotics as a general theory of *linguistic* signs, and not as a general theory of *signs* of which linguistic signs are a part, as does Peirce. The result is a quite different approach to signs. First, by making semeiotics part of linguistics, which Saussure considers a subfield of social psychology, Saussure makes semeiotics a psychological theory. Peirce, in contrast, develops semeiotics along the lines of an unpsychologistic logic grounded in phenomenology and the normative sciences. Second, Saussure makes spoken language the paradigm for all sign processes. The focus is on sound rather than vision. Peirce, with his constant emphasis on diagrammatic thinking, focuses instead on vision. Third, Saussure takes for granted many of the traditional dualisms that Peirce rejects, including the dualism between thought and language. Because of its dualistic nature it is impossible to give a Peircean reading to Saussurean semeiotics without transforming it well beyond recognition. Recall that, for Peirce, genuine triadic relations cannot be reduced to sets of dyads (Section 3.2), and Peirce sees the sign relation as a prime example of this.

By concentrating on spoken languages, Saussure arrives at a conception of the sign that is very different from Peirce's. For Saussure, languages are man-made. Linguistic signs are double-faced entities uniting not things with names, as was traditionally held, but concepts with so-called acoustic images. The former Saussure calls the signified (*signifié*), the latter the signifier (*signifiant*). Because he focuses on spoken languages, Saussure sees the connection between signified and signifier as an entirely arbitrary one. For instance, there is nothing in the acoustic image of the word "sister" that connects it with our concept of a female sibling. This arbitrariness is borne out by the fact that different languages connect very different acoustic images to the very same concept. Take, for instance, *hermana, dada,* and *soeur,* which are respectively the Spanish, Swahili, and French acoustic images for the concept of a female sibling. Based on this observation, Saussure concludes that the arbitrariness of the sign relation must be a defining characteristic of signs and the process of semeiosis. Put briefly, in their ideal form signs are conventional, meaning that insofar they are not arbitrary they must be somehow polluted. Hence, for Saussure the paradigmatic sign relation is a purely arbitrary connection of signifier and signified, and all nonarbitrary connections must either be shown to be arbitrary as well, or fall without the domain of semeiotics.

Saussure's insistence on the arbitrariness of the sign relation makes him unreceptive to natural signs—situations where something extra-linguistic is trying to tell us something. For instance, for the physicians at Cos, a high temperature, watery faeces, or crystals in the urine were *natural,* not *arbitrary* signs of disease. As a linguist, Saussure can maintain that he does not have to deal with such sign systems. However, one gets the impression that were such natural sign systems to be treated semeiotically, they would have to be assimilated to the model on which all signs are conventional, or arbitrary. This view is taken, for instance, by Louis Hjelmslev in his *Prolegomena to a Theory of Language,* for instance, Hjelmslev portrays experience as an undifferentiated and amorphous continuum in which we make "cuts" through the diacritical act of speech. These cuts are further codified in a system that is shaped by phonetic differences that allow us to distinguish one word from another. Since experience, being undifferentiated and amorphous, cannot contribute to the structure of language, meaning is generated purely contextually by similarities and differences of acoustic images. Note that it is mainly their different views regarding the phaneron (Section 3.1) that steers Hjelmslev and Peirce in different directions when developing their semeiotics.

Now if languages are wholly arbitrary systems of signs connecting concepts with acoustic images, how can we explain their stability? Experience can be of no help, because even if experience is not the undifferentiated continuum that Hjelmslev takes it to be, none of its clues could play any role in the formation or stabilization of language as this would negate the very premise we start off with, that in their ideal form languages are wholly arbitrary systems of signs. Saussure's answer is cast in terms of another famous distinction, that is, between language (*langue*) and speech (*parole*). Language is the linguistic system as a whole, like English or French, on which the language use, or speech, of individual speakers depends. According to Saussure, language, though ultimately a product of arbitrary choices, is fixed for the community that uses it. No individual, Saussure contends, can "modify in any way at all the choice that has been made; and what is more, the community itself cannot control so much as a single word; it is bound to the existing language."[6] What fixes language, for Saussure, is tradition, a tradition so strong and so pervasive that no individual or group of individuals can set out to deliberately modify it, however modestly. Hence, language is fixed, but as it is grounded merely in arbitrary connections, it is not immune from change. As Saussure puts it: "Language is radically powerless to defend itself against the forces which from one moment to the next are shifting the relationship between the signified and the signifier."[7] Traditions change over time, and occupation by a foreign nation can alter a language dramatically even in a relatively short period of time.

Briefly put, for Saussure semeiotics is a doctrine of signs, but it is a doctrine of *linguistic* signs only. These linguistic signs are arbitrary and form a structure that is independent of anything extra-linguistic and that is kept in place by the force of tradition. Others subsequently applied Saussure's doctrine of signs to nonlinguistic sign action, while leaving its main presuppositions intact. It is there that most problems lie.

5.2 Peirce's definition of the sign

Within the secondary literature, a distinction is often drawn between Peirce's early and his late semeiotics, and the relation between the two has become a subject of fierce debate. This situation emerges in part because Peirce only writes explicitly about semeiotics at the beginning and at the end of his life. This does not mean that during the period in between semeiotics is absent. Peirce writes extensively about logic, for instance, and he does so with a keen sense of speculative grammar. More generally, Peirce continues to look at many things with a semeiotic eye.

Peirce first presents his semeiotics when deriving his new list of categories in his 1867 "On a New List of Categories" (Section 3.2). About a year later, it comes to play a key role in his *Journal of Speculative Philosophy* series where he argues that we can only think in signs and that in the process we appear to ourselves as a sign as well—not a sign in addition to the thought-sign, but we literally are the thought-sign: "the word or sign which man uses *is* the man himself" (W2:241). I return to Peirce's semeiotic philosophy of mind, which features prominently in his critique of Cartesianism, later on. This chapter focuses mainly on Peirce's later semeiotics. A good understanding of Peirce's later semeiotics is hampered not only by the large amount of writings, with their constant diversions and false starts, but also because much of it is still unpublished.

Since semeiotics is the doctrine or theory of signs, the obvious question to ask is: What is a sign? Peirce spends considerable time and effort developing a definition for "sign," or *representamen* as he also called it, comparing himself at one point to the zoologist who is seeking to define "fish" (R318:52). As we saw, Peirce defines a branch of science in terms of the interests and the activities of a particular group of people (Section 1.4). On this premise the zoologist's definition of fish should be such that it best captures what ichthyologists see it as their business to study, no matter what we historically have come to associate with the word fish.

The same should hold for the concept of sign. Here too we should find that definition that best captures what semeioticians see it as their business to study. In the next chapter, we discuss Peirce's pragmatism, which is a method for clarifying our thought by developing so-called pragmatic definitions for our key concepts. It is such a definition that Peirce is looking for here as well. In this section, I discuss several of Peirce's definitions and draw out some conceptual points.

Shortly before the turn of the century, Peirce gives the following concise definition of a sign: "A sign is something which stands to somebody for something in some respect or capacity" (CP2.228). This definition is at best a very crude one. The expression "standing for" is a vague metaphor, and by stating that it stands to *somebody* Peirce opens himself up to his own criticism of confusing logic and psychology. The definition does bring out, however, that Peirce sees the sign as triadic. A sign relates three components, not just two as with Saussure's signifier and signified. The sign is a genuine triad—one that cannot be reduced to a combination of dyads (Section 3.2). This means that Peirce's logic of relatives (Section 4.6) is best equipped to deal with it.

In 1908, in a letter to the British logician Philip Jourdain, Peirce gives a more precise definition, writing that a sign is,

> anything which is on the one hand so determined (or specialized) by an object and on the other hand so determines the mind of an interpreter of it that the latter is thereby determined mediately, or indirectly, by that real object that determines the sign. (NEM 3:886)

In this letter and elsewhere Peirce names this determination of the interpreter's mind the *interpretant*. Writing to Lady Welby around the same time, Peirce describes the interpretant as the effect of the sign upon a person, immediately adding that his reference to a person is "a sop to Cerberus because I despair of making my own broader conception understood" (SS:80f). Not much later he writes:

> A Sign is a Cognizable that, on the one hand, is so determined (i.e., specialized, *bestimmt*) by something *other than itself,* called its Object . . . , while, on the other hand, it so determines some actual or potential Mind, the determination whereof I term the

Interpretant created by the Sign, that that Interpreting Mind is therein determined mediately by the Object. (EP 2:493)

In this third definition, Peirce refers to the sign as a cognizable—something capable of being known. Hence, for Peirce, signs need not to be directly perceivable by our senses, nor do they need to be actually cognized. A sign is still a sign even if there never has been, and perhaps never will be, anyone to interpret it. All the definition requires is that there is a *potential* interpretant. Elsewhere, Peirce refers to the sign even more broadly as "anything *of whatsoever mode of being,* which mediates between an object and an interpretant" (R318:81; emphasis added). In light of what is said in preceding chapters, it is tempting to say that signs are hypostatic abstractions (either *entia rationis* or *entia realis*), but Peirce does not explicitly say this. Given the relation between logic and semeiotics and Peirce's frequent criticism of psychologism in logic, his references to person and mind should be addressed, and I will do so in the next section.

Earlier, when defining logic as "formal semiotic," Peirce gives a more formal definition that is well worth including also:

A sign is something, A, which brings something, B, its *interpretant* sign, determined or created by it, into the same sort of correspondence (or a lower implied sort) with something, C, its *object*, as that in which itself stands to C. (NEM 4:54)

When describing the relations between the sign, its object, and its interpretant, Peirce's terms of choice in this definition are "determined" and "specialized." The *Century Dictionary* defines "to determine" as setting a boundary or limit, and Peirce himself composes one of its subentries: "In *logic*, to explain or limit by adding differences" (CD:1573). The same dictionary defines "to specialize" as "to limit to a particular kind of development, action, or use" (CD:5805). Thus we can say that, though any object, say a footprint on the beach, can give rise to a great variety of signs (human presence, the firmness of the sand, etc.), and though any sign can give rise to a variety of interpretations (a spouse's infidelity, the movement of the tide), each object limits, or determines, what may be a sign of it, and each sign similarly limits what may be an interpretant of it. Peirce's account further suggests that what is picked out as a sign and how it is interpreted relates to the purpose of the interpreter. An immediate question that arises is whether signs can be perfectly determinate. Peirce denies that they can (CP4.583).

Anything can be a sign as Peirce defines it. Examples are a weathervane, a cloud formation, a single word, a sentence, Gibbons' *Decline and Fall of the Roman Empire,* a dream, the entire thought-life of a person, the body of all thought, and even the universe itself. Signs can be very simple or they can be very complex. In fact, we can extract from Peirce's semeiotics the following theorem: "If any signs are connected, no matter how, the resulting system constitutes one sign" (R1476:38).

Having said something about the sign, I devote the next two sections to the interpretant and the object.

5.3 The interpretant

In the previous section, we saw that Peirce sees the sign as something that relates at once to an object and to what he calls an interpretant. Crudely put, the interpretant is the effect the sign produces. The familiar notion behind this is that of interpretation—as when we interpret someone's smile as encouraging, sarcastic, seductive, cynical, or condescending. Peirce speaks of an *interpretant* rather than of an interpreter, as he seeks to extract from our notion of interpretation only what is essential for something to act as a sign. More specifically, in line with his criticism of psychologism, he wants to keep semeiotics free from any psychological presuppositions on what the mind is and how it functions. In Chapter 2, we found that projective geometry is distinguished from topology by the introduction of a restriction that is based on our idea of a ray of light. Because of this restriction we can focus on straight lines, even though from a purely topological perspective there is no basis for singling them out. Moreover, when we practice projective geometry—like we did when determining whether the sum of the three angles of a triangle equal two right angles—we refer at no point to rays of light or the paths of particles traversing in time, and having made them into *entia rationis,* we happily move lines around, extend them where needed, use them to construct planes, and so on. Peirce seeks to do something similar for the interpretant. For instance, in his 1902 Carnegie application he explains that, "if the logician is to talk of the operations of the mind at all ... he must mean by 'mind' something quite different from the object of study of the psychologist" (NEM4:20). In a different draft of the same application he explains further that there is absolutely no reason for bringing our "peculiar feeling of consciousness" into our definition of a sign, as it "has nothing to do with the logicality of reasoning" (NEM4:54). This does not mean that consciousness, or reflexivity, plays no role at all. For instance, Peirce also states that he intends to show that "it follows from the definition of an argument, as a sign which definitely signifies its intended interpretant, that an argument must be a self-conscious sign," adding that he will "formally define this self-consciousness, without any resort to psychology or to the peculiar flavor of human self-consciousness" (RL75:217). On other occasions he uses the expression "quasi mind" (EP2:389).

Though I return to Peirce's conceptions of mind and self later (Section 9.4), some preliminary comments may help us getting a better handle on how Peirce conceives of the interpretant. In the 1860s, Peirce develops a semeiotic conception of mind. In three papers for the *Journal of Speculative Philosophy,* he argues that we can only think in signs, and, rejecting introspection, that in the process we appear to ourselves as a sign as well—not a sign *in addition* to the signs we think, but we literally are the signs we think. As Peirce puts it: "The word or sign which man uses *is* the man himself" (W2:241). Peirce does not deny that we tend to identify ourselves with our consciousness, but he adds: "This consciousness, being a mere sensation, is only a part of the *material quality* of the man-sign" (W2:240). Consciousness, Peirce admits, is used also to explain the unity in our thought, "but this unity is nothing but consistency, or the recognition of it," which is true for "every sign, so far as it is a sign" (W2:240f). Another obstacle in conceiving of the human mind as a sign, Peirce observes, is our tendency to identify ourselves with our will, meaning our ability to control the animal organism that accompanies our thought. By itself, however, this controlling power is merely a brute force; it is blind. What constitutes our self-identity is not this blind force, but the *consistency* we acquire in what we do and think.

Given this interpretation of the interpreter, we can say that the interpretant is itself a sign, or, to say the same thing, that the effect of a sign is always another sign. This is the principle of unlimited semeiosis, which plays a central role in the early Peirce: "a sign is not a sign unless it translates itself into another sign," and so on, *ad infinitum* (CP5.594).

Over time Peirce comes to realize that not every interpretant needs to be another sign, but that some interpretants are ultimate. Take an Olympic swimmer who is developing his stroke. Every experience of muscle strain or of the resistance of water is a sign to be used to perfect the stroke. When, in the end, the stroke is internalized as a habit to the point where the swimmer is no longer conscious of those muscle strains and the specific ways the water resists his motions, a sign process has terminated in an *ultimate interpretant* that is no longer itself a sign. Such an ultimate interpretant can again become the *object* of a sign, which happens when a competitor, coach, or swimsuit designer studies the stroke. But that's another matter.

When discussing the interpretant, Peirce draws two threefold divisions, one concerning the *relation* between the sign and the interpretant, and another concerning the different types of interpretants that result.

In the first division—concerning the relation between the sign and the interpretant—Peirce distinguishes between immediate, dynamic, and final interpretant. The *immediate interpretant* is "that which is necessarily brought about if the sign is to be such; it is a vague possible determination of consciousness" (R339:287r). Peirce also calls it "the immediate pertinent possible effect in its unanalyzed primitive entirety" (R339:288r); it is what is "represented, explicitly or implicitly, in the sign itself" (R339:276r); it is the interpretant that is "implied in the fact that each Sign must have its peculiar Interpretability before it gets an interpreter" (SS:111). As with any possibility, an immediate interpretant can be actualized in various ways. An interpretant that is actualized—that is, any interpretant concretely formed in a specific act of interpretation—Peirce calls a *dynamic interpretant*, even if it is merely a first hunch, a wild guess, or the product of wishful thinking. Any actual interpretation counts. Hence, this dynamic interpretant can be defined as "the actual effect produced upon a given interpreter on a given occasion in a given stage of his consideration of the sign" (R339:288r). The *final interpretant* (which Peirce also calls the normal or genuine interpretant) Peirce defines as, "the effect the Sign would produce upon any mind upon which circumstances should permit it to work out its full effect" (SS:111), or as he also puts it "the one Interpretative result to which every Interpreter is destined to come if the Sign is sufficiently considered" (id.). In the next chapter, we will see how this works out for scientific inquiry, which seems to be the situation that was foremost in Peirce's mind, and in Chapter 8 we will see how this relates to Peirce's conception of truth. At least at one point Peirce posits the final interpretant as an ideal, in that it embraces, "all that the sign could reveal concerning the Object to a sufficiently penetrating mind, being more than any possible mind, however penetrating, could conclude from it, since there is no end to the distinct conclusions that could be drawn concerning the Object from any Sign" (R339:276r). To briefly sum up the division, as does Peirce: "The immediate Interpretant is an abstraction, consisting in a Possibility. The Dynamic Interpretant is a single actual event. The Final Interpretant is that toward which the actual tends" (SS:111). In his logic notebook, Peirce also calls them the expressed, affected, and representative interpretant (R339:263r). And as Peirce further explains, the immediate, dynamic, and final interpretant "are possessed by every sign" (R339:287r).

The final interpretant must not be confused with the ultimate interpretant discussed earlier. Clearly not every ultimate interpretant—as it is there defined—meets the criteria for being a *final* interpretant, and there is no reason to assume that a final interpretant, just because it is final, must be ultimate as well. A true proposition would be a final interpretant, but it is still a sign, and hence would not be an ultimate interpretant. Peirce also deliberately omits something like the *intended interpretant*, because, "so far as the intention is betrayed in the sign, it belongs to the immediate Interpretant. So far as it is not so betrayed, it may be the Interpretant of *another* sign, but it is in no sense the interpretant of *that* sign" (R339:276r).

Peirce's threefold division raises the question whether it is still possible to misinterpret something. A few things can be said in response: a misinterpretation is still an interpretation, any dynamic interpretant, insofar as it differs from the final interpretant, is to that extent mistaken, and an immediate interpretant may suggest itself as a sign of an object while it is not a sign of that object but of another object.

In the second threefold division—the one according to the different types of interpretants that result—Peirce distinguishes between emotional, energetic, and logical interpretant. The *emotional interpretant* is the feeling produced by the sign. In some cases, this is the only significative effect the sign produces (CP5.475).

Producers of romantic movies have this down to a tee. Skillfully combining music and imagery, they can create the emotional effect even when the viewer dislikes the script or the characters. The *energetic interpretant* is an action. This can be physical, or it can be psychical, as in an exertion of attention. However, it is always a *particular* act. Finally, the *logical interpretant* is "a thought or other general sign, or a habit formed or modified" (CP5.486). This second division shows that Peirce denies that the significative effect of the sign must always be intellectual.

The three interpretants just distinguished are related in that "the logical interpretant is an effect of the energetic interpretant, in the sense in which the latter is an effect of the emotional interpretant" (CP5.486). For example, a driver who sees a child suddenly cross the street experiences a feeling of alarm, which may result in the act of breaking, all of which may result in the realization that one should be careful when driving in residential streets. Of course, not every feeling leads to action, nor do all acts give rise to thought, or to habits.

The two threefold divisions of the interpretant neither compete nor can they be reduced to one another, but they can be combined. A dynamic interpretant, for instance, can be emotional, energetic, or logical.

By making the interpretant an essential component of the sign, Peirce avoids having to make meaning a function of the intention of the sign utterer. In this way, he circumvents the problem that signs that have no utterer—like the symptoms of diseases or clouds signaling an approaching thunderstorm—would have no meaning (CP8.185). Of course one could contend that such natural signs are "uttered" by God, but Peirce rejects this option (id.).

5.4 The object

As we saw, the sign relates at once to the interpretant and to the object, the latter being, for Peirce, "anything that comes before a mind in any sense" (RL482). In the last section, we examined the relation between the sign and its interpretant, together with the various types of interpretants that can arise. In the current section, we examine the relation between the sign and its object. With regard to the object, Peirce draws a fairly traditional distinction between the object that gives rise to the sign and the object that is revealed within the sign. Peirce calls these respectively the dynamic object and the immediate object. Similar distinctions go back at least to the Stoics with their distinction between the object as it exists independently of any representation and the object as it is represented.[8]

The *immediate object* Peirce describes as "the Object as presented in the Sign" (EP2:498), "the Object as cognized in the Sign" (EP2:492), or "the Object as the sign represents it" (CP8.343). This means that the immediate object depends for its being on "the Representation of it in the Sign" (CP4.536).

The *dynamic object* refers, not to what is represented in the sign, but to what occasions this representation. It is "the Object outside of the Sign" (SS:83), or the "really efficient but not immediately present object" (CP8.343), or as Peirce also puts it, "the Reality which by some means contrives to determine the Sign to its Representation" (CP4.536). In contrast to the immediate object, the dynamic object does not depend for its being on how it is represented in any sign. The dynamic object, Peirce explains to Lady Welby, is forced upon the mind in perception, while encompassing more than perception reveals (SS:197). And he cautions her not to assume that, therefore, the dynamic object must be external to the mind.

The dynamic object has an indexical component, like when I point and say: "There is an oasis at the horizon, right there." This indexical component is not part of how the object appears in the sign. To put it differently, the immediate object—the object as it appears in the sign—cannot show me whether there really is an oasis at the horizon, whether it is a mere mirage, or whether it is the abandoned set of a Lawrence of Arabia movie. Rather, the sign indicates or hints at a dynamic object as its *raison d'être*. To ascertain what that dynamic object is, we must go beyond what appears in the sign and acquire what Peirce calls *collateral experience* (SS:83). Such collateral experience is gained when we interpret various other signs as indicating that very same dynamic object. For instance, looking at a map or traveling closer to the horizon would provide collateral experience that would confirm or disconfirm my belief that there is an oasis at the horizon. It is primarily by acquiring collateral experience that we increase our knowledge of the dynamic object. Peirce even goes a significant step further by arguing that we cannot say, without falling into absurdity, that there might be aspects of this dynamic object that are inaccessible to us *in principle*. As Peirce's defense of this stronger claim is intimately tied up with his pragmatism, I postpone a discussion of it till Chapter 7. The upshot of it is that, for Peirce, only practical considerations—such as a lack of time, money, or interest—prevent us from gathering the collateral experience we need for a complete knowledge of the dynamic object of any sign. This allows Peirce to characterize the dynamic object as follows: The dynamic object is "the Object in such relations as unlimited and final study would show it to be" (EP 2:495). Peirce occasionally calls the dynamic object the *real object,* on the ground that it is "the Object insofar as it is not modified by being represented" (R793:14). At other times, however, he rejects this usage as misleading because also a fictitious object can produce a real effect (R339:279r).

If we relate the distinction between the immediate and the dynamic object with our discussion of the interpretant in the last section, we can say that the immediate object corresponds to the sign's immediate interpretant, and that the dynamic object corresponds to the sign's final interpretant.

Though I postpone a discussion of Peirce's theory of truth to Chapter 8, a few comments can be made here. Not unsurprisingly, Peirce sees truth as the conformity of a sign to its object, and he repeatedly stresses that he really means *its* object. What is relevant here, however, is not that the sign *resembles* its object, but that the object *compels* the sign.

5.5 Three questions

The triadic relation of sign, object, and interpretant suggests three questions that should be asked with respect to the sign, namely: (1) What is the sign like when looked at in isolation? (2) How does the object determine the sign? (3) How does the sign determine the (dynamic) interpretant?

In response to the first question, Peirce gives a threefold classification, distinguishing between a tone, a token, and a type. A *token* is "an existing thing or actual historical event which serves as a sign" (R339:276r). A *type* is "a general form which can be repeated indefinitely and is in all its repetitions one and the same sign" (id.). The several instances of the word "the" on this page are all tokens of the same type, namely, the word "the" as it is being used in the English language. A *tone* is an indefinite significant character. When we italicize an instance of the word "the" for emphasis, we changed its tone. Tones are not repeatable as types are. Because each tone is unique, they have similarities at best. Though Peirce's favorite example is a linguistic one, the distinction itself isn't. For instance, a symphony considered as to its structure is a type, an actual performance of it a token, and its esthetic effect its tone. Instead of tone, Peirce also speaks of *tuone,* a blend of tune and tone, meaning "a quality of feeling which is significant, whether it be simple, like a tone, or complex, like a tune" (R339:276r). The distinction can be applied also to the mathematicians' use of diagrams discussed in Chapter 2. The diagram as the specific figure one contemplates—that is when conceived as a token with a certain tone—is read as a type by prescinding "the accidental characters that have no significance" (NEM 4:317). Peirce's tone-token-type distinction survives in an impoverished form within mainstream philosophy as the type-token distinction.

The tone-token-type distinction enables Peirce to differentiate between three types of signs: qualisigns, sinsigns, and legisigns. A *qualisign* is a tone or quality that is a sign (EP2:291). A qualisign has no identity through time. Take the experience of twice squeezing an avocado to see whether it is ripe. To say we are dealing with the same qualisign is not an issue of identity, Peirce argues, but of similarity, and the two experiences need not differ that much for them to count as different qualisigns (SS:32f). A *sinsign* is a token, which may be an actual existent thing or event, that is a sign (EP2:291). A *legisign* is a type that is a sign. Each single instance of a legisign is a token, or, as Peirce also calls it, a *replica*.

In response to the second question, how does the object determine the sign, Peirce distinguishes three types of connection: resemblance, causality, and convention. As far as the object is concerned, we must first separate the sign's immediate from its dynamic object. Regarding the sign's relation to its *immediate* object, Peirce distinguishes between the sign of a quality, the sign of an existent, and the sign a law (SS:33). With respect to the sign's relation to its *dynamic* object, Peirce distinguishes between icons, indices, and symbols. The *icon* exhibits its object through a similarity or analogy, or, more generally, the sign shares with its object a certain power of evocation. An example is "the sentiment excited by a piece of music considered as representing what the composer intended" (SS:33). The *index* exhibits its object by standing in a real relation with it, as with the symptom of a disease (id.). The *symbol,* finally, is a sign "which is determined by its dynamic object only in the sense that it will be so interpreted" (id.), for instance, by a habit, a convention, or an association of ideas. The American flag is a good example of a symbol, as its significance is wholly determined by the ideas interpretants associate with it. The three types of signs are not mutually exclusive. The famous photograph where six soldiers raise the American flag at Iwo Jima is an icon, as its form partakes in what formed it, an index, as it stands in an existential relationship with its dynamical object, and a symbol, as it has become an sign for the victory over Japan in WW2 and the sacrifice it took. Icons, indices, and symbols all come into play whenever we reason: the icon "exhibits a similarity or analogy to the subject of discourse"; the index "forces the attention to the particular object intended without describing it" (as with pronouns and proper names); the symbol "signifies its object by means of an association of ideas or habitual connection between the name and the character signified" (CP3.369).

Finally, when responding to the third question—how does the sign determine the dynamic interpretant—Peirce distinguishes three ways a sign may affect, or appeal to, the interpretant: it may present itself as a mere object for *contemplation*, as something that is "*urged* upon the interpretant by an act of insistence," or as something that is "*submitted* to its interpretant, as something the reasonableness of which will be acknowledged" (SS:34f). Put differently, the sign's interpretant can represent the sign as a sign of possibility, of actual existence, or of reason.

The three types of signs that Peirce here distinguishes are: rheme, dicent, and argument,[9] which Peirce takes to be a semeiotic rendition and broadening of the old distinction in logic of term, proposition, and argument. A *rheme* is "any sign that is not true or false" (SS:34), such as "the mortality of man" (CP4.538). A *dicent* is a sign that is "*capable* of being asserted," where an assertion is understood as "an exhibition of the fact that one subjects oneself to the penalties visited on a liar if the proposition asserted is not true" (SS:34). Consequently, a dicent is a sign "represented in its signified interpretant *as if it were* in a Real Relation to its Object. (Or as being so, if it is asserted.)" (id.). Peirce later broadens this second type to include any grammatical sentence that is intended "to have some sort of compulsive effect on the Interpreter of it," whether it be an assertion, a question, or a command (CP4.538). Peirce finally defines an *argument* as: "a sign which is represented in its signified interpretant not as a Sign of that interpretant (the conclusion) ... [but] *as if it were* a Sign of the state of the universe to which it refers, in which the premises are taken for granted" (SS:34; emphasis added). Or, as he puts it later, it is a sign "which has the Form of tending to act upon the Interpreter through his own self-control, representing a process of change in thoughts or signs, as if to induce this change in the Interpreter" (CP4.538). Earlier, Peirce defines an argument as a sign "which is understood to represent its Object in its character as Sign," which implies that in an argument thought can itself become an object of thought (EP2:292).

5.6 A classification of signs

So far we have been examining the sign in its relation to its object and its interpretant. In the process, we discovered that we must distinguish two types of objects and three types of interpretants. Also, in the last section we examined three ways a sign can represent, and the various ways they can relate to their object and their interpretants (albeit that we limited ourselves to the dynamic interpretant only). We can summarize the results from the previous section in Table 5.1.

Table 5.1 Sign Trichotomies

		1	2	3
1	A sign is:	a mere quality,	an actual existent,	a type or general law.
		qualisign	*sinsign*	*legisign*
2	A sign relates to its (dynamical) object having:	some character in itself,	some existential relation to its object,	some relation to the interpretant.
		icon	*index*	*Symbol*
3	A sign's interpretant represents the sign as a sign of:	possibility,	actuality,	reason.
		rheme	*dicent*	*argument*

For instance, the barking of a dog is a rhematic indexical sinsign of an unexpected visitor, Darwin's *Origin of Species* an argumentive indexical legisign of the principle of evolution, and a vague feeling of dread a rhematic iconic qualisign.

For Peirce, not all combinations are possible. Qualisigns can only be iconic because they cannot point at anything beyond themselves; they merely display some quality of the sign. Icons can only convey a possibility; hence they can only be rhemes. Sinsigns (where a particular object as a whole is the sign) can only relate to their object as icons or indices. As icons, they can again only be rhemes; as indices they can also be dicents. Legisigns, finally, can be icons, indices, or symbols. As icons, they can again only be rhemes. As indices, they can again only be rhemes or dicents. Finally, as symbols they can be rhemes, dicents, or arguments. This means that only legisigns that determine their objects as symbols can be interpreted as arguments. Put briefly, by first starting off from the qualities of the sign, then take into account how these different signs can be determined by their objects, and then considering how the result can determine an interpretant, Peirce comes to distinguish ten types of signs (Table 5.2).

Peirce's tenfold classification, which is a product of three trichotomies, is only the beginning. He also devises a table of 28 classes of signs, based on six trichotomies, and a table of 66 classes of signs, based on no less than ten trichotomies (EP2:481). The reduction to 66 classes of signs is considerable, as ten trichotomies can be combined in no less than 59,049 ways (id.).

What Peirce is doing here, is to establish for semeiotic—and thus for logic—something like Mendeleyev's periodic table. He gives structure to its subject matter by providing a table of elements that displays their recurring, or periodic, properties. And just like Mendeleyev's periodic table, Peirce's typology provides us with a structured way of asking questions. It allows us not only to see what sort of questions are relevant (and what sort of questions are not) but also provides us with some measure as to the completeness of our inquiry.

Table 5.2 Peirce's Tenfold Classification of Signs (CP2.254–63)

	The sign's phenomenological quality	How that sign could have been determined by its object	How the result can determine an interpretant	Example (given by Peirce)
1	Qualisign	As an icon	As a rheme	A feeling of "red"
2	Sinsign	As an icon	As a rheme	An individual diagram
3		As an index	As a rheme	A spontaneous cry
4			As a dicent	A weathercock
5	Legisign	As an icon	As a rheme	A diagram, apart from its factual individuality
6		As an index	As a rheme	A demonstrative pronoun
7			As a dicent	A street cry (identifying the individual by tone, theme)
8		As a symbol	As a rheme	A common noun
9			As a dicent	A proposition (in the conventional sense)
10			As an argument	A syllogism

CHAPTER SIX

Philosophy of science

With his background in philosophy, his interest in logic, and his extensive experience as a practicing scientist, Peirce is well equipped to write about what we today call the philosophy of science. When he speaks of scientific inquiry, what he has in mind is inquiry into positive fact, where the latter is conceived at its most basic level, antecedent even to any metaphysical commitments. Conform Peirce's division of the sciences, we have recourse only to phenomenology, the normative sciences insofar we have discussed them (being part of speculative rhetoric, philosophy of science still falls within the domain of the normative sciences), and mathematics. Recall further that when Peirce talks about science he is thinking of something much broader than what the term currently refers to, especially within the Anglo-Saxon world. He means to include any positive inquiry engaged in with the aim of ascertaining the facts. It includes history, cultural anthropology, the work of a homicide detective, as well as particle physics and molecular biology.

For Peirce, inquiry always starts from the situation we actually find ourselves in, with all the doubts and beliefs that come with it. Peirce rejects that we can extract from this some sort of indubitable foundation upon which we can build our edifice of knowledge. This search for an indubitable epistemic ground is a common fixture in modern philosophy, whether it comes in the guise of an *ego cogito*, clear and distinct ideas, simple ideas, or sense data. In his *Meditations Concerning First Philosophy*, Descartes envisions himself sitting in his evening gown next to the fireplace, undisturbed by passions, trying to ascertain whether any of his beliefs are truly beyond doubt. In the process, Descartes discovers that the very act of doubting implies that he himself is a thinking thing. This causes him to conclude that we can be absolutely certain that we have a mind whenever we are thinking, and on this indubitable foundation he rebuilds his knowledge. Descartes' methodology has been called one of universal doubt. Peirce rejects this method because it is not inspired by real doubt, but only by pretend doubt: "genuine doubt does not talk of beginning with doubting. The pragmatist knows that doubt is an art which has to be acquired with difficulty; and his genuine doubts will go much further than those of any Cartesian" (R845:10). Peirce refers to this as his doctrine of *critical common sensism*: "there are some propositions that a man, as a fact, does not doubt; and what he does not doubt, he can, at most, make but a futile attempt to criticize. The test of doubt and belief is conduct. No same man doubts that fire would burn his fingers; for if he did he would put his hand in the flame, in order to satisfy his doubt" (R318:271). In sum, Peirce turns Descartes' method of doubt on its head. We should not begin with universal doubt and see which beliefs can withstand all doubt, but accept all the beliefs we have as long as we are willing to give up any single one of them when faced with contrary evidence, a position he dubs *fallibilism,* and *anti-cock-sure-ism*. Overall, Peirce's approach is closer to Darwin than to Descartes. Human inquiry is continuous with how animals explore their environment and captured in a homeostatic model where there is a constant gravitation to a relatively stable set of beliefs.

6.1 The sole purpose of inquiry is to fix belief

Peirce's two most widely read papers are "The Fixation of Belief" and "How to Make Our Ideas Clear." They are the first of six papers that Peirce wrote for the *Popular Science Monthly* under the general heading "Illustrations of the Logic of Science." In the first, Peirce presents his theory of inquiry, in the second his theory of meaning, which is later known as pragmatism. The papers feature prominently in Peirce's teaching at Johns Hopkins, and throughout his life they continue to play a central role. The current chapter centers largely on the first paper; the next chapter focuses on the second.

As noted, inquiry starts for Peirce always from the situation we find ourselves in, with all the passions, doubts, fears, prejudices, affinities, beliefs, desires, etc. that we bring with us. Peirce thereby rejects one of the key presuppositions of modern philosophy, that of epistemic agnosticism. This agnosticism is exemplified in Descartes' claim in the *Meditations* that he is inquiring while he is "undisturbed by passions," and in the empiricists' prohibition of admitting anything that ventures beyond a supposedly neutral description and classification of observations. In Peirce's view such a presupposition is unrealistic.

Having established that we can only begin with the beliefs and doubts we actually have, Peirce proceeds with the familiar observation that there is a felt difference between a state of belief and a state of doubt. The first is a serene and satisfactory one; the second is marked by uneasiness and dissatisfaction. In fact, this dissatisfaction makes us so uneasy that once doubt sets in we do our utmost best to return to a state of belief, whether it is a new belief or a return to the belief we had before. In the process anything goes, as long as it frees us from the discomfort of doubt and brings us back to a state of belief. Moreover, since all we are after is to regain a state of belief, our searching comes to an end the very moment we no longer doubt. Because of this, Peirce concludes that the formation of belief is *the sole object* of inquiry, scientific or otherwise.

Before turning to the various ways belief can be (re)gained, something should be said about what Peirce means by *belief*. Peirce's 1902 Carnegie application contains perhaps his fullest account. There he takes belief to express "any kind of holding for true or acceptance of a representation" (NEM4:39). What he has in mind, though, is not a state of consciousness, but "a habit established in the believer's nature, in consequence of which he would act, should occasion present itself, in certain ways" (id.). Peirce immediately qualifies, though, that not every habit is a belief, but only those "with which the believer is deliberatively satisfied" (id.). This implies that the believer is somehow aware of the habit, and does not struggle against it. Moreover, whereas habits are generally contracted through repetition, one can acquire a belief "by merely imagining the situation and imagining what would be our experience and what our conduct in such a situation; and this mere imagination at once establishes such a habit that if the imagined case were realized we should really behave in that way" (NEM4:39f). In short, for Peirce, beliefs are habits of deliberate action that one endorses as one's own, including wholly imaginary lines of conduct (CP5.538). Or, as he puts it elsewhere, "a belief consists in the deliberate acceptance of a proposition as a basis of conduct" (CP8.337). This latter formulation also brings out that whereas there is a strong sense that belief comes in degrees (new discoveries can strengthen or weaken a belief) there is also an absoluteness to it. You either believe that God exists, that abortion is immoral, that the earth is motionless, and so on, or you don't. This absoluteness enters with the deliberate acceptance of the belief, which is nothing other than a moral commitment of the believer. In agreement with this, and with the normative conception of logic discussed in Chapter 4, Peirce describes *reasoning* as "such fixation of one belief by another as is reasonable, deliberate, self-controlled" (CP5.440).

6.2 Four ways of fixing belief

In "The Fixation of Belief," Peirce distinguishes four ways of settling belief, or opinion: the method of tenacity, the method of authority, the a priori method, and the method of science. *The method of tenacity* is entirely defensive in nature. One fixes the beliefs one already has by tenaciously holding on to them, dismissing off-hand any evidence against them. However, when faced with opposing beliefs or recalcitrant facts, this method provides no guidance on how to settle the issue. Consequently, Peirce argues, doubt inevitably creeps in. Especially in today's diverse society where we are frequently confronted with views very different from ours, this method is unlikely to give us stable belief. Nonetheless, there are still heroic efforts, like that of Vicki Frost, an evangelical Christian who sued her daughter's elementary school because in teaching her to respect the views of others they diverted her from "the one true way."[1] Most cases, however, are not that deliberate. Being in denial, making one's beliefs unfalsifiable in the way Popper accused the Marxists of doing,[2] or having them float in an ever-changing quicksand of vague generalizations and half-baked opinions, are also examples of this method.

The second method is *the method of authority*. Here society, in the form of the Church, State, or otherwise, enforces certain beliefs by manipulating information, or by rewarding those that advocate the accepted belief structure while silencing those that seek to undermine it. The method of authority is far more powerful and stable than the first, and as Peirce points out, one that has a long and impressive track record. However, as no institution can regulate opinion on every subject, this method too is destined to cause doubt. A famous example is the swinging lamp in the cathedral of Pisa that awoke the young church-going Galileo's interest in physics, an interest that was instrumental in ending the authoritatively fixed belief that the earth is the unmoving center of the universe. For the second method, it is not necessary that a believer realize that his belief is grounded in authority. Good propaganda makes people freely believe what the authorities want them to believe, and good advertising makes people freely choose a product because of what its manufacturer says about it.

The third way of fixing belief operates by the sanction of thought alone. Peirce calls this *the a priori method*. In this method, we try to settle belief by latching on to what seems agreeable to reason. The long-held belief that heavy bodies fall faster than light ones is a good example of something that was believed simply because it somehow "made sense." Some prime adherents of this third method are René Descartes, who grounded our beliefs in clear and distinct ideas, Kant who grounded them in sensory and pure intuition, and Hegel, who as Peirce puts it, "simply launches his boat into the current of thought and allows himself to be carried wherever that current leads" (CP5.382n). More generally, we can say that the third method appeals particularly to those who see a strong divide between reason and passions, and who then consider it our main task to free our thought from the pernicious influence of the passions. The idea is that, when undisturbed by passions, reason unfolds wholly according to its own laws, which are the laws of logic.

In contrast to the first two ways of fixing belief, where the mechanism through which a belief is fixed is wholly external to the belief that is being fixed—in principle any belief can be fixed by tenacity or authority if the force is strong enough—here the *content* of the belief steers the process of fixation. Consequently, in contrast to the first two methods—which are hardly methods of inquiry— the a priori method, like the scientific method that I discuss next, is properly a method of inquiry. Interestingly, this third method builds, albeit in a superficial manner, on the view discussed above that logic is ultimately an offshoot of esthetics (Section 4.1).

The problem with the third method, Peirce argues, is that what we find agreeable to reason is not very stable. "The opinions which today seem most unshakable," he writes, "are found tomorrow to be out of fashion," so much so that the most unshakable beliefs of one generation become so unbelievable to those that come next that they find it altogether incomprehensible that people at once genuinely believed them (CP5.382n). Hence, like the first two methods, the a priori method is unlikely to net lasting belief. It is rather to be expected, Peirce writes, that the pendulum of taste will endlessly swing back and forth between a limited number of alternatives (W3:253).

In sum, none of the three methods are likely to cause a secure belief. Their failure, however, does suggest what type of method to look for. In the methods discussed so far, it is the inquirer, either as an individual or as part of a group, who determines what is to be believed and what is not. This causes Peirce to conclude that we should seek to fix our beliefs by something that is independent of what you or I or any group in particular may think them to be. Peirce calls this *the method of science*.

Peirce's insistence on this fourth method is in part due to his own experience as a scientist. It made him acutely aware that the confrontation with hard fact has proven many purportedly self-evident theories false. Take the claim Robert Grosseteste made in the early thirteenth century, that when a beam of light enters a different medium it bends at a ratio of 2:1. This phenomenon can be observed by partially submerging a straight stick in a clear pond. Grosseteste came to his conclusion because it seemed the most reasonable one to him. The law of reflection had already taken the simplest ratio, 1:1, and 2:1 was the next simplest one. In 1621, the Dutch astronomer Willebrord Snell showed that Grosseteste was mistaken. After extensive observation, Snell found that the ratio varies depending on how fast light travels through each medium and the angle at which it hits the other medium. This is quite different from what Grosseteste took it to be *a priori*.

In contrast to the first three methods, the method of science requires that Peirce gives an account of how this independent reality relates to our thoughts. This is no easy matter. In fact, philosophers have been so unsuccessful in this, that Kant termed it a scandal.[3] I will say more about this relation when discussing Peirce's conceptions of truth and reality in Chapter 8. For the moment it suffices to say that, as far as the method of science is concerned the idea of external reality to which our beliefs must conform is only *a regulative hypothesis*, and Peirce presents four reasons why he thinks this hypothesis is justified. First, though inquiry cannot *prove* it, it cannot disprove it either, so that "the method and the conception on which it is based remain ever in harmony" (W3:254). Put differently, applying the scientific method never causes us to doubt the hypothesis. Second, the dissatisfaction that constitutes doubt already contains "a vague concession that there is some *one* thing to which a proposition should conform" (id.). In other words, all who take their doubt seriously share the hypothesis, so that there is no social impulse that causes us to doubt it. Third, the method of science is widely used, and we only cease to use it when we do not know how to apply it (id.). Fourth, the method has been wildly successful, so that our experience of applying the method does not cause us to doubt the hypothesis either (id.). It is unlikely that these four reasons will appease the hardened sceptic, but they are not meant to. According to Peirce, the sceptic's doubts are not genuine; they are merely feigned doubts occasioned by unrealistic demands that are in turn inspired by fallacious, often metaphysically inspired, preconceptions.

Peirce's account of the method of science runs roughly as follows: when a group of inquirers study something that is independent of what they think it to be, this independence ensures that eventually their beliefs gravitate to one another and become settled in a shared belief, assuming the inquiry continues long enough to allow this to happen. In this way, the method of science seeks to take into account *both* the impact of experience and the beliefs of others. This method has proven to be very successful in fixing belief in many areas. Take our current beliefs about the solar system, about the causes of diseases, or about the stresses and strains that need to be reckoned with when building a suspension bridge or skyscraper. In fact, we can say that most people today entertain a broadly scientific worldview, meaning that the method of science has a great impact on how their ideas are fixed. This is true even though we participate in it mostly vicariously, simply trusting what others say when we believe their pronouncements are supported by science.

Peirce's views on science have their roots in his experience as a practicing scientist. For much of his life he worked as a geodesist. That he was active in the earth sciences instead of particle physics is significant. Although philosophers of science often consider the latter the paradigm of science, the idea that there is a world out there that provides us with stubborn facts we have to hypothesize about is much more pronounced in the earth sciences. Take Arizona's Barringer Crater. Initially, it was believed to be of volcanic origin, a belief that came easily, not only because of the crater's shape but also because of its proximity to the San Francisco volcanic field. Moreover, fairly convincing albeit hypothetical evidence suggested that a meteorite could not have caused the crater. In 1903, Daniel Barringer challenged this view on the ground that the surrounding plains were covered with large oxidized iron meteorite fragments. He further conjectured that the bulk of the meteorite must be buried under the crater floor and spent the next 27 years looking for it. Barringer never found the meteor, a fact explained by the currently accepted hypothesis that the strength of the impact caused most of the meteorite to vaporize. In 1960, Eugene Shoemaker confirmed Barringer's impact hypothesis after discovering the presence of stishovite, a rare form of silicon dioxide that is found only where quartz-bearing rocks have been severely shocked by instantaneous overpressure, and the presence of which cannot be explained by volcanic action. The impact hypothesis also explains why the layers immediately exterior to the rim are stacked opposite to how they are found normally. This brief account illustrates that there is a strong sense in which Grove Karl Gilbert, who advocated the volcano hypothesis, Daniel Barringer, and Eugene Shoemaker all studied the same object, that this object is independent of what any of these scientists thought it to be, and that if our inquiry into this object continues long enough, its stubborn presence will force our opinions about it eventually to converge.

Now, is the scientific method clearly superior to the other three? If fixing belief is truly all that matters, what is the man of science to say to someone who successfully applies the method of tenacity? This becomes especially pertinent when the application of the scientific method, rather than simply fixing belief, occasions new doubts.

It seems that the scientist can say in response that believing that something is the case entails believing the belief is stable—that it does not collapse under the smallest pressure—and that we can differentiate between various methods of fixing belief in terms of the stability of the beliefs generated by it. A related advantage of the method of science is that even though we may sense that our beliefs are not final, we can find solace in the fact that when some of our beliefs are shaken we have a reliable procedure in place for dealing with our doubts the moment they surface. Doubt becomes much more manageable when we have a general sense of how to alleviate it, especially when it concerns issues that are not of immediate and vital concern. Recall that Peirce restricts the sciences of discovery to theoretical sciences only. In short, good arguments can be given by those adhering to the method of science on why that method is to be preferred, even when confronted by others who successfully fix their beliefs with the first three methods.

Peirce, however, wants to go further and argue that by using the scientific method we can fix our belief permanently, and not only that, but that in doing so we discover how things really are. Peirce's defense of this stronger claim is grounded in his pragmatism, which is the subject of the next two chapters. According to Peirce's pragmatism the meaning of any term is restricted to the conception it conveys. On this view, calling something incognizable is to utter something that is entirely without meaning—a mere *flatus vocis*. From this Peirce concludes that whatever is meant by "reality" must be "cognizable in some degree, and so is of the nature of a cognition" (W2:238). I return to this in Section 7.3. In other words, Peirce's response to the problem of the external world is to embrace a form of idealism on which to be is to be cognizable. For Peirce, this is an *objective* idealism, as he grounds it in a *social* epistemology that centers on the *community* of inquirers. In the process of inquiry the (subjective) idiosyncrasies of the individual inquirers are filtered out, and assuming inquiry continues long enough, they are eventually replaced by objective truth. What enables Peirce to do this is his pragmatic conception of truth, on which the truth regarding any question is the opinion that eventually would be reached by the community of inquirers, assuming the inquiry is not cut short for extraneous reasons, whether it is a lack of funds, the extirpation of the human race, or the death of the entire universe. Peirce's pragmatic conception of truth is discussed in Chapter 8.

6.3 The demarcation of science

In the last section, we saw that the crucial difference between the method of science and the other three methods is that in the method of science belief is ultimately fixed by something not under our control. The example of the Barringer Crater shows how the stubborn opposition of hard fact—or, as Peirce's has it, its secondness—features within scientific inquiry. We also saw that, for Peirce, the starting point of any inquiry is the beliefs we happen to have at the time. There is no Archimedean point or indubitable foundation we can first go to and subsequently proceed from. Instead we approach any inquiry, scientific or other, with all our biases and predispositions, many of which are products of the other three methods of fixing belief. Because of this, Peirce insists that science is an inherently social affair. The interaction with fellow inquirers is crucial for filtering out the various idiosyncrasies that individual inquirers bring to the table—it allows us, as he puts it, "to grind off the arbitrary and the individualistic character of thought" (R969:3f). The solitary genius so favored by novelists, like Shelley's Frankenstein or Stevenson's Dr Jekyll, is to Peirce not a scientist at all. In fact, not even his observations count: "one man's experience is nothing if it stands alone. If he sees what others cannot see, we call it hallucination" (CP5.402n).

In contrast to the first three methods, error plays a central role in science, as it is precisely when we are wrong that we are given the strongest evidence that there is a world out there that is independent of what we may think it to be, and with which we are somehow in direct contact. Hence, there is an important sense in which error is to be encouraged rather than avoided. This too speaks to the idea that science is a communal enterprise, and one that should involve people with different backgrounds, inclinations, and talents, so that the greatest variety of angles is explored. Part of what is at play here are Peirce's conceptions of self and mind, which are decidedly anti-Cartesian. Peirce defines the private self not in terms of anything exquisite or divine, but in terms of error and ignorance. What makes our private selves unique is that we differ from others in that we are wrong about different things and that we are ignorant about different things. Hence, for Peirce, scientific inquiry—which seeks to alleviate error and ignorance—is in essence a process of self-effacement. I return to Peirce's conceptions of mind and self in Section 9.4.

The idea of reconciling idiosyncrasies in the face of stubborn fact raises the question whether there is some special way for doing this that makes this reconciliation scientific. There are clearly unscientific ways of reconciling our differences, such as the method of authority outlined above or by taking a vote. Some have argued that what demarcates science from non-science is precisely that the former uses the "scientific method" and the latter doesn't, after which the challenge becomes that of articulating this method. Peirce denies that there is a single scientific method, as if there is one shoe that must fit them all. Instead, he argues, "every science must develop its own method out of the natural reason of man" (EP2:78). Peirce, moreover, rejects that the scientific method is a priori in that it can be developed antecedent to and independently of its application. The methods used in science are themselves accomplishments of scientific inquiry. In fact, scientific methods are to Peirce so much a product of the actual practice of science that he not only considers each major advance in science a lesson in logic, but also rejects the notion that ratiocination is something that takes place within the mind. As already noted in Section 4.2, Peirce credits the French chemist Antoine Lavoisier with making his alembics and cucurbits instruments of thought, thereby inaugurating "a new conception of reasoning as something which was to be done with one's eyes open, in manipulating real things instead of words and fancies" (W3:243f). The link with action is crucial. In a chapter entitled "What is the Use of Consciousness," written for his 1894 logic book *How to Reason,* Peirce warns that "intelligence does not consist in feeling intelligently but in acting so that one's deeds are concentrated upon result" (R406:2). Science is not an exercise in contemplation, but must be practiced—and this is true even for theoretical science. And as we saw in Chapter 2 this is true even for the pure mathematician, who is in the business of constructing diagrams, experimenting upon them, and observing the results. The idea that reasoning involves experiment also brings us back to the notion that logic, including scientific reasoning, is a normative enterprise. Experimentation involves *voluntary* action that we deliberately approve of, and, as Peirce rightly observes, "the approval of a voluntary act is a moral approval" (R312:28).

Conformant with the above, Peirce draws a distinction between rope and chain reasoning. In his *Rules for the Direction of the Mind,*

Descartes likened scientific arguments to long syllogistic chains that connect our conclusions with an indubitable foundation. Besides problems with the idea of such a foundation, Peirce believes that this analogy is misguided. Scientific arguments are rather like ropes. They resemble a multitude of threads that—though each of them is weak when taken in isolation—can be woven together to make a sturdy rope (W2:213). When scientific reasoning is likened to a chain, a single mistake causes the entire chain to break. It also suggests that for each step in the argument we should opt for the one that forges the strongest link, and ignore whatever else may have a bearing upon that same connection. As opposed to Descartes' chain, which becomes useless the moment a single link gives way (at least until that particular link is repaired) a rope remains fully intact should one or even several of its fibers snap (even when they are never replaced), especially when new fibers are constantly woven in. By taking this course, Peirce takes recourse to the multifarious arguments of the schoolmen in a manner that allows the greatest plurality of insights, approaches, methodologies, and the like to contribute to the growth of knowledge.

In conclusion, we can say that Peirce denies that there is a single scientific method that can be identified before the inquiry begins and to which it is subsequently applied. Instead, the practice of science gives rise to the development of various methods, and how well they do when they are being applied determines their continued use.

Now if there is no such thing as a method that can be used to determine what constitutes science and what does not, how then does Peirce demarcate science from non-science? Peirce's answer is that what distinguishes science from other cognitive enterprises is not the *method* used, but the *attitude* with which it is engaged in. An inquiry is scientific when it is engaged in with a genuine desire to learn, freed from any predisposition as to what the answer should be. It is the search for knowledge for knowledge's sake, not for some other reason, whether it is to find a cure for cancer, reduce greenhouse gases, or promote one's fame or career. It should be added, though, that Peirce is talking of the sciences of discovery only. The situation is different for the practical sciences, the aim of which is not to discover how things really are no matter what, but to further certain preset goals, including the reduction of greenhouse gases and finding a cure for cancer. According to Peirce, when in our inquiry we are inspired by the scientific attitude, this will cause us to develop or appropriate the methods we need. In other words, defining science in terms of its method is to put the cart before the horse.

Peirce summarizes his position in what he calls the first rule of reason: "in order to learn you must desire to learn and in so desiring not be satisfied with what you already incline to think" (RLT:178). To this he adds as an important corollary the imperative: "Do not block the road of inquiry" (id.). There are many ways this road can be blocked, such as the already mentioned references to the unknowable, maintaining that some beliefs are self-evident, an overly aggressive demand for foundations, requiring that all science is modeled after the hard sciences, and an exaggerated emphasis on certitude or exactness. This first rule of reason is an imperative of speculative rhetoric. Peirce distinguishes other imperatives of speculative rhetoric as well. Most prominently there are the pragmatic maxim which is discussed in the next chapter, his theory of the economy of research, and synechism, the view that whenever possible we should presume things continuous.

As we saw in Chapter 4, however, Peirce distinguishes a general methodology for scientific inquiry, which he extracts from the three basic modes of argumentation (abduction, deduction, and induction; Section 4.5). This raises the question whether this could be taken as the scientific method, and hence give us a principle of demarcation. To recapitulate, when we hit upon a surprising phenomenon, we should begin by searching for a hypothesis that would explain it. Peirce calls the process through which we reach such a hypothesis *abduction*. When, using the regulative principle of the economy of research we have decided on a hypothesis, we use *deduction* to extract all that can be derived from that hypothesis in conjunction with our other beliefs—in particular we should seek to establish what observations or experimental results follow from the truth of the hypothesis. Finally, we put the hypothesis to the test, using *induction*. For Peirce, this strategy puts certain constraints on the type of hypotheses one is to look for. As he explains in a letter to Cassius J. Keyser:

> In order that a hypothesis should be useful to science, it should have so definite a character that the leading characteristics of the phenomena should be *necessary consequences,* or at least, hardly avoidable consequences, of its truth; so that in case the hypothesis be false, it should furnish ample handles for its refutation.[4]

The approach outlined is not unlike Karl Popper's methodology of conjecture and refutation, even including the demand that hypotheses be falsifiable. There is at least one important difference, though, and this is that Peirce also allows hypotheses to be verified, a position he can take because of his fallibilism and his theory about the ideal end of inquiry (Section 8.2). To the above, we can further add that like the more targeted methods discussed earlier, this general methodology should also be taken as an (empirical) outcome of scientific inquiry, not as something that is externally (or a priori) imposed on it. Apart from the fact that Peirce need not commit himself to the view that all scientific inquiry must follow this pattern, it seems that even an inquiry that does follow this method *only* qualifies as science if it is engaged in with a scientific attitude, that is, with a genuine and unconditional desire to learn. Now one could counter that if one were to conscientiously follow the method of abduction, deduction, and induction one would ipso facto exemplify this desire to learn, as any other motivations would be extraneous to it. But it is not clear whether this is so. The bullshitter, for one, can go through all the motions of the prescribed method, not caring anything about what comes out of it. Hence, even if it is true that all scientific inquiry, and *only* scientific inquiry, follows this method, it still puts the cart before the horse as it is precisely the commitment to an unconditional desire to learn that determines whether the method just outlined is scientific or not, and not the other way around. Hence, what distinguishes science from non-science is still the attitude with which the inquiry is engaged in, not the method(s) that are being used.

Peirce's conception of scientific inquiry causes him to reject Coleridge's definition of science as systematized knowledge, which is the standard definition at the time. In its place, Peirce defines science as "a branch of study, sincerely aiming at the discovery of the true, and deliberately selecting its methods in the light of the knowledge which man has attained and published" (R18:02), from which he concludes that:

> Science is to mean for us a mode of life whose single animating purpose is to find out the real truth, which pursues this purpose by a well-considered method, founded on thorough acquaintance with such scientific results already ascertained by others as may be available, and which seeks coöperation in the hope that the

truth may be found, if not by any of the actual inquirers, yet ultimately by those who come after them and who shall make use of their results. It makes no difference how imperfect a man's knowledge may be, how mixed with error and prejudice; from the moment that he engages in an inquiry in the spirit described, that which occupies him is science, as the word will here be used. (CP7.54)

Hence, rather than a dead body of established fact, science is a living process that should be defined, not in terms of the bits of knowledge that are picked up on the way, but in terms of "the devoted, well-considered, life pursuit of knowledge" (R1126:8). Because of this "it is not sufficient to find the general conditions of the truth of a representation. It is necessary further to study the laws of the development of scientific representations" (R787:10).

CHAPTER SEVEN

Pragmatism

Legend has it that pragmatism originated in the early 1870s when a small group of mostly young men from Cambridge, Massachusetts, gathered to talk philosophy. With an ironic and defiant air, they called themselves—in honor of a discipline they considered obsolete—The Metaphysical Club. No records of their meetings survive, but from correspondence and publications it is clear that they rejected how philosophy was practiced at the time. As such they were part of a broader shift that was taking place at Harvard (Section 1.1). Besides Peirce, the group included William James, John Fiske, Chauncey Wright, and the lawyers Oliver Wendell Holmes Jr and Nicholas St John Green. Central to their discussions was Alexander Bain's definition of belief as "that upon which a man is prepared to act." When that definition is granted, Peirce writes later, pragmatism follows almost immediately as its natural outcome. Peirce's theory of inquiry, discussed in the last chapter, is clearly conceived with Bain's definition in mind. However, when people refer to Peirce as the father of pragmatism, they are rather thinking of a maxim Peirce enunciated in the second paper, "How to Make Our Ideas Clear," by which he sought to provide a better way of making our ideas clear than was thus far suggested by logicians. Perhaps, this focus on the maxim is due to William James, who called attention to it in his 1898 Berkeley Union address "Philosophical Conceptions and Practical Results."[1] However, it is also because of its foundational nature. The maxim leaves no intellectual conception, philosophic or scientific, untouched, and as a result it causes the entire fabric of thought to shift in significant ways.

Thanks mostly to William James, pragmatism takes off at the end of the nineteenth century. Among its main proponents, we find Ferdinand Schiller, John Dewey, George Herbert Mead, and C. I. Lewis. In Italy, a particularly vocal albeit short-lived group of pragmatists emerges, centering around Giovanni Papini, Giuseppe Prezzolini, Giovanni Vailati, and Mario Calderoni.[2] Though Peirce tried to join the bandwagon that he had inadvertently set in motion, his views, deeply critical of the other pragmatists, failed to become mainstream. Not affiliated with a university, living in relative isolation, and not publishing in mainstream venues all worked against him.

Pragmatism was not well received by the philosophic community. To contrast his views with what he considers the vacuous mental machinations of armchair philosophers, James famously identifies truth with the cash value of our ideas. This proves a powerful but dangerous metaphor. It makes it easy for others to dismiss pragmatism offhand as a shallow apology of crass American capitalism, and this is precisely what happens. Peirce and James, however, explicitly deny that pragmatism is anything new, or even particularly American. They rather see it as the conscious and systematic adoption of a method that philosophers have been practicing from antiquity onward. Peirce even boldly declares the newness of a philosophical idea as one of the surest signs of its falsity. And to show pragmatism's noble pedigree, he enlists even Jesus among the pragmatists, reading the latter's "ye may know them by their fruit" as an early version of his pragmatic maxim. James seeks to bring home the same point when he subtitles his book called *Pragmatism* with *A New Name for Some Old Ways of Thinking*.

According to James' biographer, Ralph Barton Perry, "the modern movement known as pragmatism is largely the result of James's misunderstanding of Peirce."[3] However, when we look closely at the early works of both, and take into account how over the years James continues to influence Peirce, this view cannot be maintained. It seems, rather, that by the time Peirce publishes his famous maxim, James' emphasis on conduct and practicalness is already firmly in place. In other words, in contrast to what Perry writes, James does not misinterpret Peirce's pragmatism, but their views represent two different strands of pragmatism, each having its origin in the discussions that took place within The Metaphysical Club in the early 1870s. The situation gets a bit more complicated by the end of the nineteenth century when James makes pragmatism explicitly the pivot of his thought, referring to Peirce as its originator. James' nominalistic interpretation of Peirce quickly gains popularity. To distance himself from this, Peirce names his doctrine *pragmaticism*, a word he believes is ugly enough to safeguard it from kidnappers (CP5.414). It is to this view that the current chapter is devoted.

7.1 "How to Make Our Ideas Clear"

Whoever engages in philosophy, Peirce argues, brings to it "a stock of confused ideas upon the subject" (R953:10), something that is true also for other intellectual endeavors. Because of this, "there has to be for each question we attack a serious, preliminary business of rendering our ideas clear" (id.). Peirce's 1878 "How to Make Our Ideas Clear" is a sustained attempt at developing a methodology for doing this. Peirce's idea of what an idea is comes close to the definition he writes for the *Century Dictionary*: "an immediate object of thought—that is, what one feels when one feels, or fancies when one fancies, or thinks when one thinks, and, in short, whatever is in one's understanding and directly present to cognitive consciousness" (CD:2973). Recall Peirce's notion of the phaneron discussed in Section 3.1. When Peirce speaks of making our ideas clear, he is in effect talking about the process of extracting something from the phaneron so that it optimally serves some cognitive purpose. It is logic, as the third and highest of the normative sciences, that tells us what this cognitive purpose is, or should be, and how to reach for it. As we will see, that purpose is in essence the attainment of an opinion that no future inquiry can unsettle.

In "How to Make Our Ideas Clear," Peirce distinguishes three grades of clearness. An idea reaches the first grade when it "will be recognized whenever it is met with, and so that no other will be mistaken for it" (W3:258). This first grade can be exemplified by a seasoned pawnshop owner's idea of gold. His idea of gold allows him to recognize that an object is made of gold the moment he sees it, and it allows him to interpret sentences that contain the word "gold." All that is needed to attain this first grade of clearness is familiarity with gold objects. Though this first grade of clearness is primarily a sensuous clearness (R254:6), it need not be narrowly empirical. One can obtain a clear idea of unicorns, electrons, or the trinity by becoming familiar with how these concepts feature in our language and culture. For instance, we have a clear idea of a unicorn when we can identify *references* to unicorns as references to *unicorns*, as opposed to, say, references to centaurs, horses, or elasmotheriums and when we can generate references to unicorns that are generally interpreted by others as references to unicorns.

Merely having familiarity with an idea, however, is in Peirce's view not sufficient for the precision and logical security that is typically required in science and philosophy. The second grade of clearness seeks to accommodate for this. It is reached when the idea is not merely clear but also contains nothing that is not clear. We attain this second grade when we provide "an abstract logical analysis of it into its ultimate elements, or as complete an analysis as we can compass" (CP6.481). The definition of gold as the chemical element with atomic number 79 is an example of this. Here, the abstract definition steers our understanding of the concept. That is to say, whatever has atomic number 79 has to be gold, no matter what the pawnshop owner thinks or says it is. In fact, some things identified as gold at the first grade of clearness may fail the definition, whereas others meet the definition even though they were not identified as gold at the first grade. Analytic philosophers typically seek to attain the second grade of clearness for the concepts they use.

A problem with abstract definitions, however, is that they become disconnected from experience. With his third grade of clearness, Peirce seeks to accommodate for this by returning to the world of experience while retaining the precision gained at the second grade. Peirce famously casts this third grade in what is now called the pragmatic maxim:

> Consider what effects, which might conceivably have practical bearings, we conceive the object of our conception to have. Then, our conception of these effects is the whole of our conception of the object. (W3:266)

Unless the maxim shows a conception to be vacuous, application of the pragmatic maxim to ideas at the second grade of clearness renders what Peirce calls a *pragmatistic definition*, which he defines as, "a definition by means of characters that might conceivably influence rational conduct" (CD 11:348). In his Syllabus for the 1903 Lowell lectures, Peirce gives as an example the following pragmatistic definition of lithium:

> If you look into a textbook of chemistry for a definition of *lithium*, you may be told that it is that element whose atomic weight is 7 very nearly. But if the author has a more logical mind he will tell you that if you search among minerals that are vitreous, translucent, grey or white, very hard, brittle, and insoluble, for one which imparts a crimson tinge to an unluminous flame, this mineral being triturated with lime or witherite rats-bane, and then fused, can be partly dissolved in muriatic acid; and if this solution be evaporated, and the residue be extracted with sulphuric acid, and duly purified, it can be converted by ordinary methods into a chloride, which being obtained in the solid state, fused, and electrolyzed with half a dozen powerful cells, will yield a globule of a pinkish silvery metal that will float on gasolene; and the material of that is a specimen of lithium. (CP2.330)

This definition tells you what lithium is "by prescribing what you are to do to gain a perceptual acquaintance with the object of the word" (id.), with the understanding that this is what lithium means and nothing more.

The definition of lithium shows that pragmatistic definitions are open-ended. Over time, we may come to know much more about lithium, and that will force us to expand or refine our definition. In this way, what our terms mean, like the methods of inquiry discussed in Chapter 6, is a *product* of inquiry, and not something that is determined independent of and antecedent to inquiry. It indicates further that *if* inquiry can be conceived as a process through which we converge to a final opinion, the meaning of the terms used to express that opinion will similarly converge to reflect their final pragmatistic definition. Or, to express it semeiotically (Section 5.4), a series of dynamic interpretants eventually turns into a final interpretant, or "the effect the Sign would produce upon any mind upon which circumstances should permit it to work out its full effect" (SS:111).

Peirce is careful to point out, however, that "a mere jumble of particulars" is only the crudest species of a concept (CP7.467).

Rather, "a concept is the living influence upon us of a *diagram*, or *icon*, with whose several parts are connected in thought an equal number of feelings or ideas" (id.). To say that a concept is *significant*, Peirce writes elsewhere, is to say that it is "creative of living mind" (R339:443).

Though Peirce plays with the idea of adding higher grades of clearness—mostly inspired by a too restrictive reading of his own maxim—he eventually settles on three grades of clearness. For instance, toward the end of his life, in an article for *The Hibbert Journal* called "A Neglected Argument for the Reality of God," Peirce summarizes his position as follows:

> To acquire full mastery of that meaning it is requisite, in the first place, to learn to recognize the concept under every disguise, through extensive familiarity with instances of it. But this, after all, does not imply any true understanding of it; so that it is further requisite that we should make an abstract logical analysis of it into its ultimate elements, or as complete an analysis as we can compass. But, even so, we may still be without any living comprehension of it; and the only way to complete our knowledge of its nature is to discover and recognize just what general habits of conduct a belief in the truth of the concept (of any conceivable subject, and under any conceivable circumstances) would reasonably develop. (EP2:447f)

This passage shows both the relation between the three grades of clearness and their respective functions.

A question still to be asked is why these consequences must be *practical*? In what we have seen, Peirce is clearly speaking of the theoretical sciences, not the practical sciences. So, why practical consequences, rather than, say, experience, or sense impressions, as with the empiricists? To address this question, we must return to our discussion of logic. In Chapter 4, I showed that Peirce considers logic as a normative science that takes its cues from ethics and esthetics. Logic studies our deliberate thinking insofar it is aimed at representing something, where "representing" is to be taken very broadly; it studies thought insofar as it is subject to self-control with the aim of developing good habits of reasoning. In this context, Peirce's focus on practical consequences comes naturally, as it makes us focus on those consequences that have implications for what we can, will, or should do. This approach to science also ties in with a change that has been taking place within the sciences themselves. Even the theoretical sciences are no longer purely spectatorial in that they confine themselves wholly to understanding what presents itself in nature. Instead, scientists are increasingly aiming to create phenomena. A classic example is Robert Boyle's air pump, the aim of which was to bring about a phenomenon that had never been observed in nature—and the possibility of which was denied by many—namely a vacuum.

Peirce further limits the applicability of the maxim explicitly to *intellectual* concepts, which, as Peirce observes, are general. This means that we must look for a mental element that is general also. Peirce identifies two of them, desires and habits, and opts for the latter. Consequently, for an idea to be intellectually significant it must at least conceivably result in a general effect upon conduct—that is, the creation, change, or reinforcement of a habit.[4] Peirce thereby denies that experience or sense impressions can generate meaning all by themselves. What is needed is the development (or the reinforcement) of a habit. As Peirce writes to Howes Norris, "the only sort of real meaning that can attach to a general is the conception of a general resolve to behave according to some principle" (NEM3:946). Consequently, "the only real significance of a general term lies in the general behaviour which it implies" (id.).

Peirce is thus careful to observe that the practical consequences he has in mind should not be interpreted in terms of action if this means the mere exercise of brute force. As he writes shortly after the turn of the century: "while I still insist that the meaning of anything lies in what it may bring to pass, I can no longer admit that action is a final end. On the contrary, action without an ulterior end is a mere spasm" (R873:36). What is aimed for is not the mere exercise of brute force, which plays only at the level of secondness, but to further the development of reasonableness, which plays at the level of thirdness.

Peirce's conception of pragmatism thus hinges quite heavily on the notion of habit. As Peirce explains to his editor Paul Carus, we have reached pragmatic clearness when we have "a clear conception of that *Habit of Conduct* in which a given concept would work out its actualization."[5] In general, habits, or dispositions to act, need not be conscious or even consciously formed. Moreover, we do not really control how they change over time and, as our bad habits painfully show us, neither can we shed them simply by an act of will. Furthermore, many of the habits we have are social—they are products of our environment more than of our selves. Honesty, for instance, is not the private possession of a person, but a working adaptation of personal aspirations to social forces. We can even go so far as to say that habits shape us more than that we shape our habits. In fact, the *logica utens* discussed in Section 4.2 is also formed in this way. At the same time, we do deliberately form or shape habits, and it is for this that the normative science of logic—*logica docens*—aims to provide us guidance.

Now where does this all leave us with regard to the question of the meaning of the words we use? Like many of our habits, these too are social habits that are only partly under our control. "The meaning of a word," Peirce writes, "really lies in the way in which it might, in a proper position in a proposition believed, tend to mould the conduct of a person into conformity to that to which it is itself moulded" (R464:26). Or, as he puts it to Kehler: "*[B]elieving, real* genuine belief, consists in a habit with which one is contented and which one usually recognizes (though not always) this habit consisting in the general fact that under certain circumstances one would act in a definite way, and would be content to do so" (NEM3:191). In agreement with this, Peirce defines pragmatism as "the doctrine *that the* conceivable *practical consequences* (i.e. consequences for rational conduct) *completely exhaust the* INTELLECTUAL *meaning of any concept.*"[6]

7.2 Proving pragmatism

Peirce goes well beyond his fellow pragmatists by requiring that pragmatism be proven. The reason is that even though pragmatism has proven itself capable of resolving many difficult issues, it is a familiar fact to scientists and philosophers alike that simple rules often "have had to be greatly complicated in the further progress of science" (EP2:139). Put differently, it is quite safe to say that, as a rule of thumb, our conception of the conceivable practical consequences of a concept is the meaning of that concept, but can we truly say that no concept whatsoever has any meaning *apart* from those consequences? Are there really no strange cases that require the rule to be tweaked a little? Since genuine doubt regarding the maxim can be raised, and since the maxim profoundly affects all we may inquire into by (re)defining even our most basic conceptions, Peirce believes that it is only appropriate to demand a proof.

When Peirce is talking of a proof, he is not thinking of an argument in the old rationalist sense, where each proposition follows by necessity from those that precede it. Rather, he envisions the proof as an instance of rope reasoning (Section 6.3):

> Just as a civil engineer, before erecting a bridge, a ship, or a house, will think of the different properties of all materials, and will use no iron, stone, or cement, that has not been subjected to tests; and will put them together in ways minutely considered, so, in constructing the doctrine of pragmatism the properties of all indecomposable concepts were examined and the ways in which they could be compounded. Then the purpose of the proposed doctrine having been analyzed, it was constructed out of the appropriate concepts so as to fulfill that purpose. In this way, the truth of it was proved. There are subsidiary confirmations of its truth; but it is believed that there is no other independent way of strictly proving it. (CP 5.5)

Any such proof should begin with phaneroscopy and then run through the normative sciences. Besides convincing us of the truth of pragmatism, such a proof has the added advantage of showing "how the different properties of the subject-matter ... are related to one another, and how the whole plan of studying them hangs together" (NEM2:65).

In Chapter 5, we saw that Peirce sees semeiotics as covering either the whole of logic or speculative grammar only. For the purpose of grounding pragmatism, the latter more modest view is all we need, as pragmatism follows straightforwardly from Peirce's definition of the sign, which falls within the purview of speculative grammar. In Chapter 5, we saw that Peirce defined the sign as anything that is so determined by an object and so determines an interpreter that the latter is thereby determined mediately by the object that determines the sign (NEM3:886). From this, Peirce argues, we can conclude that "the meaning of any sign is its rightful *effect*" (R339:348r). I also noted that the application of the pragmatic maxim is restricted to intellectual concepts only. Hence, we must establish where to classify intellectual concepts in Peirce's division of signs. As intellectual concepts are by nature general, they cannot be icons or indices. This leaves symbols as our only option. Now, Peirce defines symbols as signs that signify their object "by means of an association of ideas or habitual connection between the name and the character signified" (CP3.369). The following definition of a symbol makes the tie with pragmatism even clearer:

> The being of a symbol consists in the real fact that something surely *will be* experienced if certain conditions be satisfied. Namely, it will influence the thought and conduct of its interpreter. Every word is a symbol. Every sentence is a symbol. Every book is a symbol. Every representamen [or sign] depending upon conventions is a symbol. (CP4.447)

Though Peirce initially restricts the connections established by symbols to conventions only, he later also includes "natural dispositions" (CP4.531). Pragmatism can thus be seen as the doctrine of the meaning of a certain type of symbols. Or, if we want to be a bit more precise and follow Peirce's tenfold classification of signs (Section 5.7), pragmatism seeks to determine the meaning of those rhematic indexical legisigns that are employed as intellectual concepts. Peirce further writes that: "the *meaning* of any speech, writing, or other sign is its translation into a sign more convenient for the purposes of thought" (NEM2:251)—a process that, as we saw, ideally terminates in a final interpretant. In this manner, Peirce grounds pragmatism not in any laws of metaphysics or psychology, but in "a logical and non-psychological study of the essential nature of signs" (NEM2:520f). As he put it to a former student: "Pragmatism is one of the results of my study of the formal laws of signs, a study guided by mathematics and by the familiar facts of everyday experience and by no other science whatever."[7] All the above is fortified further by Peirce's view, hinted at in Chapter 5, that all thought is in signs, so that there cannot be any conceptions that are not signs.

As we saw in Section 4.3, Peirce reduces all arguments to three basic forms (deduction, induction, and abduction) and subsequently fits them together into one very general method of inquiry (Section 6.3). Now, if pragmatism is a maxim of logic, as Peirce claims it is, then the question to ask is: Where or how does pragmatism feature in this trifold division and in this general method? In his

1903 Harvard Lectures, Peirce explicitly identifies pragmatism as the logic of abduction (EP2:234f). Recall that abduction is the process of hypothesis formation (Section 4.5). Though, as we saw, Peirce attributes our ability to find good hypotheses in part to our instinct of guessing right, the *logic* of abduction must by definition fall within our deliberate control, meaning that it can be subjected to normative principles like the pragmatic maxim. Based on the above, we can say that the pragmatic maxim evaluates hypotheses in terms of their conceivable practical consequences. It determines what hypotheses mean in terms of their practical consequences, reveals hypotheses that have no practical consequences whatsoever, and shows which hypotheses are identical to which—even though they may be formulated very differently—because there is no difference in their conceivable practical consequences. In this way, Peirce provides a rule for the admissibility of hypotheses that is broader than the requirement that hypotheses be testable (as Carnap argued) or falsifiable (as Popper argued), and that also covers considerations of the economy of research. Now if we add to this Peirce's dictum that we should never block the road of inquiry (Section 6.3), it follows that we should not put any restrictions on abduction beyond what is absolutely necessary. This causes Peirce to conclude that "a maxim which looks only to possibly practical considerations will not need any supplement in order to exclude any hypotheses as inadmissible," so that "the maxim of pragmatism, if true, fully *covers* the entire logic of abduction" (EP2:234f). Peirce next continues by showing that pragmatism cannot affect induction or deduction, so that its only logical import is that it covers the logic of abduction.

Peirce's pragmatic maxim is often compared with the verification principle proposed by the Logical Empiricists in the first half of the twentieth century. For instance, in his "Two Dogmas of Empiricism," Quine writes: "The verification theory of meaning, which has been conspicuous in the literature from Peirce onward, is that the meaning of a statement is the method of empirically confirming or infirming it."[8] The aim behind the verification principle is to weed out profound-sounding but meaningless statements by requiring that all statements we assert are either tautologies or reducible to simple observation statements using a system of logic that is itself tautological. The last requirement ensures that the rules of derivation, which are not empirical, can be accepted as meaningful. Wielding this principle, Logical Empiricists have declared as meaningless all religious, metaphysical, aesthetic, and ethical statements. In addition, Logical Empiricists saw themselves forced to reject many scientific statements and many statements about the past.

Though there are certain similarities between the pragmatic maxim and the verification principle, they are amply overshadowed by the differences. In Chapter 4, we saw that Peirce's conception of logic is far broader than that of the Logical Empiricists, and there is much in Peirce to suggest that he rejects the analytic-synthetic distinction as the Logical Empiricists envisioned it. In the current chapter, we saw further that Peirce also rejects any reading of his maxim that makes the practical effects consist in *particular* acts or *particular* observations, and the latter is the be-all and end-all of the verification principle. The pragmatic maxim must also not be confused with the famous phrase, commonly attributed to Wittgenstein, that "meaning is use." This phrase, typically quoted out of context, comes from the following claim by Wittgenstein: "For a *large* class of cases—though not for all—in which we employ the word 'meaning' it can be defined thus: the meaning of a word is its use in the language."[9] The idea behind this is that the meaning of many words can be established through an empirical study of its actual use within a particular linguistic community. This is very different from what Peirce has in mind.

7.3 Some applications of the pragmatic maxim

To illustrate how the maxim works, I shall discuss a few examples before going into a more detailed analysis of the conceptions of truth and reality in the next chapter. An event that is presumed to take place during the Eucharist is the transubstantiation of wine and bread into the blood and body of Christ. According to Catholic dogma, the bread and wine literally change into the body and blood of Christ, and they do so without any modification of their physical characteristics. That is to say, after the transubstantiation, the bread still has the same texture as before and the wine still tastes like regular wine.

It is not difficult to obtain a clear and distinct idea of transubstantiation, especially if one admits the Aristotelian substance-attribute distinction. For Aristotle, a substance is an individual object we can point at, like this man or that horse. In grammar, this substance takes the role of the subject of a sentence. Attributes are qualities that can be predicated of a substance. For instance, we can attribute the quality of whiteness to a horse by saying "This horse is white." It will be easily granted that the substance-attribute distinction allows us to form the conception of transformation. In a transformation, say from caterpillar to butterfly, the substance (i.e. the individual object) remains exactly the same even if many of its qualities change.

Along the same line, we can form a conception of transubstantiation. Here, the exact opposite occurs. This time it is the substance that changes while the qualities, or attributes, remain exactly the same. This means that after the transubstantiation we have a different subject, even though there has not been any change in qualities. The idea of transubstantiation allows one to say that after the Eucharist one is literally eating and drinking the flesh and blood of Christ—that is, the substance of Christ—even though it still looks, feels, and tastes like ordinary bread and wine.

Recalling Peirce's three grades of clearness, we can say that for transubstantiation we reached the second grade of clearness here. However, and because of it, we only have an abstract definition. When, subsequently, we apply the pragmatic maxim to it, as does Peirce, the entire concept is quickly revealed as meaningless (W3:265f). As we saw, on the pragmatic maxim the meaning of any concept is nothing but its conceivable practical effects. Now, *by definition* our conception of transubstantiation cannot have any such practical effects since we derive our knowledge of any substance from its qualities and the very idea of transubstantiation presupposes that there is no change in qualities at all. Since it makes no conceivable practical difference whether transubstantiation takes place or not, Peirce argues, the concept of transubstantiation is wholly meaningless.

The pragmatic maxim similarly reveals as meaningless the skeptic's brain-in-a-vat hypothesis. On this hypothesis, a modern day variant on Descartes' evil demon argument, you might for all you know be a brain-in-a-vat. So while you may think you are running a marathon, neither the roads, trees, and competitors you see nor the muscle ache you feel is real. Instead, it's all part of a complex illusion created by a computer that feeds all this directly into your brain which is quietly floating in a dark container in some laboratory. Accepting for the sake of the argument the rather bizarre notion of a flawless computer—a presupposition required to make the deception complete—it is clear from the pragmatic maxim that the question whether or not you are a brain-in-a-vat is entirely meaningless as there is no conceivable practical difference between the two options. Hence, the skeptic's suggestion that you might be a brain in a vat, and that all you perceive is not real, is as vacuous as the idea of transubstantiation.

Pragmatism further reveals that references to absolutely incognizable things in themselves, as Kant does, or to Herbert Spencer's "unknowable," are entirely meaningless. True, we can formulate a definition at the second grade of clearness, but no matter how we do it, it contains a direct denial of the very possibility of forming a conception of it in terms of its practical consequences. Hence, application of the pragmatic maxim shows the definition to be vacuous. Now one could object by saying that positing unknowable causes for our cognitions still has explanatory value, and that this suffices for constituting a practical difference. Peirce dismisses this on the ground that any such explanation would be directly self-nullifying, as it comes down to "explaining" something by calling it inexplicable, which is not an explanation at all. It only urges us to stop looking, so that it serves no other purpose than to block the road of inquiry. The consequence of Peirce's pragmatic analysis of the concept of unknowable causes is, as we saw in Section 6.2, that Peirce embraces a form of objective idealism. In short, the application of the normative principles of logic to the very general empirical question as to what causes our sense impressions leads us to an objective idealist metaphysics. Logic here informs metaphysics. I return to this in Chapter 8.

An immediate concern one might have is that, like the verification principle referred to earlier, the maxim throws out too much as meaningless. For the mathematician Peirce incommensurables form an obvious candidate. It is stated that we cannot precisely express the ratio of the circumference of a circle to its diameter. To accommodate for this, mathematicians simply introduced a new quantity, π, such that the circumference equals πd (where d is the circle's diameter). This π is said to be incommensurable with the integers. That is to say, we can approximate the value of π in integers—and in 2010 Alexander Yee and Shigeru Kondo calculated it up to no less than the five trillion digits—but we cannot state it precisely. *Practically*, however, there seems no difference between calling π commensurable or incommensurable (CP5.32). To draw, for instance, a circle the size of a hydrogen atom using integers only, we only need to know the first 39 digits of π.[10] Does this mean the distinction is meaningless? Peirce denies that it is, and he does so precisely by drawing attention to conceivable practical consequences: It gives the practical advice that it is useless to search for the exact expression of the diameter as a rational fraction of the circumference (CP5.539). It enables us to say that π differs from any expression of it in integers by some assignable finite (and commensurable) quantity that can be revealed in further calculation (CP5.204). It allows us to conceptually differentiate a circle from regular polygons that have their vertices joined by straight radii to their center—assuming the number of vertices is finite (CP5.203), etc. In sum, the distinction has distinct and identifiable practical consequences.

Peirce's most contentious example is that of hardness, as it is this example that is responsible for the nominalistic reading of the maxim by William James and others (including, at times, Peirce himself). In good pragmatic fashion, Peirce calls a substance hard when it "will not be scratched by many other substances," and he adds that therein lies "the whole conception of this quality" (W3:226)—meaning that there is nothing more to it than that. So far so good. Peirce goes on, however, by saying that, "there is absolutely no difference between a hard thing and a soft thing so long as they are not brought to the test" (id.). Hence, strictly speaking it would not be false to say that diamonds that are never put to the test are soft. Peirce's struggle with "hardness" marks a moment in his evolution from nominalism to realism. Though there are strong realist tendencies in "How to Make Our Ideas Clear," and a realist reading of the pragmatic maxim comes naturally, Peirce is still sticking to some nominalist positions, including a denial that mere possibilities can be real. Though Peirce later explicitly revises his earlier application of the maxim to "hardness" (see, e.g. EP2:356f), this did little to undo the damage that was already done.

Though pragmatism is sometimes made out to be a metaphysical doctrine—even if only in the limited sense of providing a basic worldview—it is good to remember that, to Peirce, pragmatism remains strictly a regulative principle in the normative science of logic, or, to be more precise, in speculative rhetoric. However, this means that it tells you what criteria need to be met for any intellectual conception you intend to use to have meaning. And as this also applies to our most basic conceptions, the principle of pragmatism leads in that sense to a pragmatist worldview. It is important to realize, though, that applying the principle is not optional, so that any so-called alternative view must be defunct at its very basic level. As Peirce writes to Charles August Strong: "I regard any metaphysics not based on pragmatism as a mere form of words to which no meaning whatever can be attached."[11] In the next chapter, we examine how the application of pragmatism changes what we can mean with "truth" and "reality."

CHAPTER EIGHT

Truth and reality

In this chapter, we apply the pragmatic maxim to two concepts: truth and reality. The result is a pragmatic theory of truth and a position that Peirce comes to call Extreme Scholastic Realism. Both illustrate the far-reaching effect of applying the maxim to fundamental philosophical concepts. Application of the maxim to these two concepts also brings us within the realm of metaphysics. To best understand what Peirce means by metaphysics, we should see where he places it in his classification of the sciences. Metaphysics, for Peirce, is the third and highest branch of philosophy. Philosophy, we saw, is the study of the most basic facts of everyday life. More precisely, as the discipline coming next after logic, metaphysics concerns the first application of logic. Keeping in mind that we should not try to settle a priori what can be tested by experience (Section 5.2), as that would block the road of inquiry rather than opening it up, Peirce confines metaphysics to the study of what can be established independent of any specific experiences. Briefly put, metaphysics consists in the application of the regulative laws of logic to the universe, proceeding from the assumption that the universe "has an explanation, the function of which, like that of every other logical explanation, is to unify its observed variety" (CP1.487). Since, for Peirce, philosophy deals only with "so much of truth as can be inferred from common experience" (CP1.184), metaphysics only looks at the universe at its most basic level and does so with the aim of formulating a general account, or *Weltanshauung*, that can form a basis for the special sciences. It considers questions such as, is everything determined, can there be any strictly individual existence, is time real, are time and space continuous, is there a difference (other than one of degree) between fact and fancy, etc. According to Peirce, we cannot avoid having a metaphysics, we can only fail to make it explicit, in which case we end up taking rather crude metaphysical views for granted without even being aware of it.

Peirce's placement of metaphysics in his division of the sciences further shows that it cannot ground its principles in the special sciences; they can only be grounded in mathematics, phaneroscopy, and the normative sciences. This is not to deny that the special sciences cannot provide mathematics and philosophy with fresh material to contemplate, and in fact they often do. For instance, problems encountered in physics and economics have resulted in mathematical models that, once they are sufficiently generalized by the mathematician, are used by logicians and metaphysicians.

By situating metaphysics within the sciences, Peirce makes it clear that metaphysics is not exempt from the logic of science. On the contrary, logic, understood as the theory of right reasoning, is crucial to metaphysics. Our instincts and intuitions, Peirce argues, are shaped by a long history of the human species engaging with its environment. The problem with metaphysical questions is that in answering them we tend to rely on these instincts and intuitions, even though such types of questions are far removed from the circumstances that shaped our instincts and intuitions. For instance, in our daily lives, we are intimately familiar with the concept of time. We can schedule a dental appointment, say that the government was slow to react to a natural disaster, estimate when a pregnant woman gives birth, etc. But the situation is very different when we ponder questions about the origin of the universe (was time created with it, or did time somehow "exist" already), or when we speak of time as being infinite (a view that commits us to the far from intuitive idea that there are as many millennia as there are seconds). Without the help of our intuitions, and without there being any direct repercussions to even the most grossly mistaken views, metaphysicians are in desperate need of logic. In sum, rather than rejecting all metaphysics outright, as the positivists tried to do, Peirce calls for *a scientific metaphysics*, a discipline that is grounded in phaneroscopy, steeped in logic, mathematical to the core, and engaged in with the scientific attitude.

As noted, Peirce considers it the purpose of metaphysics to develop a *Weltanschauung* that can become the basis for the special sciences; or, to put it differently, to "study the most general features of reality and real objects" (CP6.6). With this in mind metaphysics can be divided into: *general metaphysics*, or ontology, which focuses on the question of reality; *physical metaphysics*, which concentrates on questions of time, space, natural laws, etc.; and *psychical metaphysics*, which concentrates on questions of mind and God (EP2:259f). The current chapter is devoted to general metaphysics, more specifically the question of reality and its relation to truth, existence, and possibility. The next chapter is devoted to several questions in physical and psychical metaphysics.

8.1 Getting clear on truth and reality

In our daily lives, we use the terms truth and reality with perfect confidence. We can safely say that for them we have attained the first grade of clearness. However, specifying with precision what we mean by calling a belief or statement true or by calling something real has proven quite problematic. For instance, for the concept of truth the dominant attempts are captured in the correspondence theory of truth and the coherence theory of truth, both of which have significant if not fatal flaws. In "How to Make Our Ideas Clear," Peirce does not directly apply the pragmatic maxim to the concept of truth. Instead, he applies it to the concept of reality. Now, if we call a statement true when its immediate object is real, as does Peirce (R958:205; Section 5.4), then we can plausibly say that once Peirce attains the second grade of clearness for the concept of reality, the second grade of clearness for the concept of truth follows easily. So let's discuss first the concept of reality.

Peirce believes he has found an adequate definition of reality of which we can say that it attains the second grade of clearness in that it delineates clearly and unambiguously what is real and what is not. This definition, which Peirce ascribes to Duns Scotus, runs as follows: The real is what is independent of what you, or I, or anyone in particular may think it to be. On this definition, Hamlet is not real, as he is clearly a product of what one particular person, William Shakespeare, thought him to be. Also mirages and bent sticks are not real, as they depend for what they are on what we think them to be (though the general phenomenon of the breaking of light might be real on this definition).

There are several observations to be made about the definition Peirce extracts from Scotus. First, it does not seek to define the term reality in terms of equally abstract terms such as existence and actuality, as is often done. For instance, the *Oxford English Dictionary*—which substantiates its definitions in part by delineating the history of the usage of the words it defines—defines "reality" as "the aggregate of real things *or existences*," and as "the quality of being real or having *an actual existence*" (emphases added). It similarly defines the use of the adjective real, as "having an objective existence; actually existing physically as a thing," or "actually existing or present as a state or quality of things."[1] Compared to such definitions, the definition favored by Peirce has the advantage that it does not commit us to treating reality and existence as virtual synonyms, nor does it require us to see "reality" as a mode of being, which is how the dictionary defines "existence," or as applying only to things. This allows us to say, as does Peirce, that there are real natural laws (meaning that they are not merely *entia rationis*) without having to commit ourselves to the view that natural laws *exist*—a commitment that invites all sorts of trouble, as natural laws are evidently very different from particular objects. On Peirce's definition, to pronounce something real only commits us to saying that it is independent of what anyone in particular—or any group in particular—may think it to be. External existence is one way that something can be real, but it need not be the only way. That is to say, Scotus' definition provides the conceptual space for calling some non-existents as real.

The definition further allows Peirce to maintain that mental events are real, and that this is so even if their objects are not. For instance, the objects that appear in a dream are not real, as they depend for what they are on what the dreamer dreams them to be. But the dream itself and the fact that those objects appeared to the dreamer are real, as they are what they are independently of what the dreamer, or anyone else, may think them to be.

This brings us to a third point, namely, the possibility of reals that depend for what they are on the state of our thought. On Peirce's definition, the objects of our thoughts are real when they are independent of what you, or I, or anyone in particular thinks them to be, *even* if those objects are mental constructions. Take the four-color theorem in mathematics. It is easy to see that you only need two colors to paint the squares of a chessboard such that any two squares sharing an edge have a different color. But what if you want to color a map with seven countries that are all shaped differently? And how many colors would you need for a map of a hundred countries? Such questions can be generalized by asking whether there is a minimum number of colors sufficient for coloring a map of any number of countries, no matter how they are shaped, so that no two countries with the same color share a border. The answer, quite remarkably, is only twice what you need to color a chessboard. In other words, there is no map possible for which you would need more than four colors to color it in. Now this problem, the argument, and its conclusion are all products of the mind, while the conclusion is inescapable in that it is independent of what anyone in particular may think it to be.[2] Hence, the four-color theorem is not merely a mental construct conjured up by a handful of mathematicians, but it is also real. However, unless we throw in some form of Platonism, it is also clear that there would be no four-color theorem without some thought process of which it is the conclusion. To restate this in more general terms, to say that something is real is not meant to imply that it is independent of *all* thought, but *only* of what you, I, anyone, or any group *in particular* may think about it or may think it to be.

As the above suggests, the definition enables us to draw the following helpful distinction. We can distinguish between (1) what is independent of what you, or I, or anyone in particular may think it to be, and (2) what is independent of what you, or I, or anyone in particular may think about anything. The four-color theorem meets the first criterion, and hence we can call it real, but it fails the second criterion in that it requires that at least some people think about the map-coloring problem. In contrast, if during a stroll we are suddenly struck against the back of our head, this brute fact is *not only* independent of what we may think about it (we cannot, as it were "think it away") but *also* independent of what anyone may think about anything. No matter what we do or do not think about, the opposition experienced in the blow against the back of the head remains unaffected. In line with this, Peirce comes to associate existence with such brute opposition, or secondness (Section 3.2).

As shown in the previous chapter, the third grade of clearness is obtained by applying the pragmatic maxim to the definition that constitutes the second grade of clearness, as that contains our most precise rendition of the concept. If we apply the pragmatic maxim to

Scotus' definition, our conception of reality becomes the conceivable practical bearings that we conceive real objects—that is, those objects that are independent of what you, or I, or anyone in particular thinks them to be—to have. Now the *only* intellectual effect such objects *can* have upon us, Peirce claims, is to produce belief. Therefore, *if* our conception of these effects is the whole of our conception of "real object," as the pragmatic maxim asserts it is, then the *belief* these real objects *can* effect upon us is our whole conception of those real objects. Consequently, "reality" can mean nothing *other* than the object of permanently settled belief or opinion.

8.2 Truth as the end of inquiry

Returning to the claim that a cognition is true when its immediate object is real, we can extract from the above a pragmatic definition of truth. On this definition, truth is nothing more, but also nothing less, than permanently settled belief or opinion. As Peirce puts it in "How to Make Our Ideas Clear": "The opinion which is fated to be ultimately agreed to by all who investigate, is what we mean by the truth, and the object represented in this opinion is the real" (W3:273). The idea behind this is "that every intelligible question whatever is susceptible in its own nature of receiving a definitive and satisfactory answer, if it be sufficiently investigated by observation and reasoning" (W4:545f), and that definitive and satisfactory answer is also the truth in the matter.

This should not be interpreted as the empirical prediction that inquiry into any question that somehow allows for an answer will eventually cause us to agree on what that answer is. Rather, it should be interpreted as the claim that "truth" and "the opinion which is fated to be ultimately agreed to by all who investigate" are synonyms (W3:273). In other words, Peirce is arguing that we cannot mean anything with "truth" *other* than the opinion we would eventually converge upon in an inquiry that is sufficiently open and continues sufficiently long to allow for the idiosyncrasies of the individual inquirers to be filtered out (Section 6.3). In other words, when I claim that it is true that there was once life on Mars, I am committing myself to the view that were this question to be inquired into by an indefinite community of investigators all of whom are inspired by the scientific attitude (Section 6.3), there would emerge, in the long run, a settled opinion that there was once life on Mars; that is to say, an opinion that no subsequent inquiry interested in solving that same question can undermine. As Peirce puts it, "the truth of the proposition that Caesar crossed the Rubicon consists in the fact that the further we push our archaeological and other studies, the more strongly will that conclusion force itself on our minds forever—or would do so, if study were to go on forever" (CP5.565). This must not be interpreted to imply that whatever happened in the past (Caesar physically crossing the Rubicon) depends on what future inquirers will have to say about it, as that would clearly put the cart before the horse.

The language of Peirce's semeiotics may be helpful in unraveling the issue (Chapter 5). The historical event of Caesar crossing the Rubicon is here cast as a dynamic object, signs of which enter human consciousness in the guise of immediate interpretants. Now, the claim that is being made is that if these immediate interpretants were to be inquired into long enough, they would eventually gravitate toward a final interpretant. Hence, again in the vocabulary of Peirce's semeiotics, when I say that it is true that Caesar crossed the Rubicon, I am claiming that the immediate interpretant of the dynamical object is also its final interpretant. In other words, it is not because something becomes an object of the final opinion that it is real, but it is because something is real (i.e. independent of what you or I or anyone in particular may think it to be) that it can become an object of a final opinion. This also means that it is not necessary that a final opinion be actually reached. It suffices that the situation is such that *were* inquiry pursued long enough by an indefinite community of inquirers, a final agreement—one that no subsequent inquiry could undermine—*would* eventually emerge. Though Peirce is initially reluctant to accept such a reading, after first assuring himself that possibilities can be real he allows this final agreement to be read in terms of a subjunctive conditional—something that is captured in the add-on phrase in the quotation given above: "or *would* do so, if study *were* to go on forever" (id., emphasis added).

Application of the pragmatic maxim thus allows us to derive the following pragmatic definition of truth when applied to propositions:

> Proposition P is true if and only if, if P were to be inquired into long enough by a sufficiently large community of investigators, this inquiry would result in a permanently settled belief that P.

The idea is that this ultimate belief is reached when all that could be inquired into were inquired into so that no future inquiry can possibly reveal anything new of it. This means that no future inquiry can show it to be false or cast any doubt on it. Consequently, this ultimate belief, or this final opinion, is a permanently settled belief. The locution "by an indefinite community of inquirers" is essential for ensuring that any distorting elements that may result from the peculiarities of the individual inquirers, such as a propensity for conspiracy theories, a general distrust of mathematics, or a desire to interpret everything as part of the grand scheme of an all-powerful and benevolent God, are filtered out. To further illustrate his point, Peirce gives the example of a deaf and a blind man who both witness a murder: "One hears a man declare he means to kill another, hears the report of the pistol, and hears the victim cry; the other sees the murder done" (W2:468). Although the sensations of the two witnesses are altogether different, Peirce argues, should they discuss what they perceived sufficiently long, "their final conclusions, the thought the remotest from sense, will be identical and free from the one-sidedness of their idiosyncrasies" (id.).

Though initially Peirce says we are fated to reach such a final opinion, he later sees it rather as a regulative ideal or a necessary presupposition of inquiry. The idea that we are *fated* to reach a final opinion comes from the recognition that there is nothing any individual or group of individuals can do to modify this opinion, or prevent it from being reached (W3:273). By taking this position, Peirce aims to express that this final opinion is not of our own making—one that could have been different had we wished so—but that it is something we are predestined to discover.

In part in response to *Monist* editor Paul Carus, who saw in it a commitment to determinism, Peirce stops talking about the final opinion as something we are *fated* to reach, maintaining instead that whenever we engage in inquiry we do so with the *hope* that it will lead to a final opinion. Inquiry, Peirce argues, is guided by the hope that to every question "there is an answer, which can be called the answer, that is, the final answer . . . which sufficient inquiry will compel us to accept" (CP4.61). To deny this (i.e. to raise a question and declare it unanswerable) is not to inquire, but to block inquiry. Hence, Peirce labels it a fundamental axiom of logic that "every intelligible question whatever is susceptible in its own nature of receiving a definitive and satisfactory answer, if it be sufficiently investigated by observation and reasoning" (W4:545f).

Peirce's shift away from talking about the final opinion as something we are fated to reach is also related to his move toward a subjunctive reading of the pragmatic definition of truth. We cannot really say that we are fated to reach a final opinion, when it is clear from the outset that for many questions finding an answer will take far more time than the human race can reasonably be said to have left, and that for some questions we have lost our chance of finding the answer. It is furthermore related to Peirce's increased focus on logic as a normative science, and his emphasis on self-control.

It is important to note that Peirce's conception of truth does not commit him to say that at the end of inquiry we will find one super story that we could call "the truth," which would contain the last word on all there is to know about life, the universe, and everything. Peirce's aim is far more modest, as the following analogy makes clear:

> The fact that I try to get well of each given bodily malady I may suffer from, is no argument that I am cherishing any hope to escape from *every* malady that I may ever suffer from. So the fact that I try to find the truth in respect to each doubt that presents itself involves no assumption on my part that there is any real truth about *all* questions. (R787:11)

Just like when in sickness we concentrate on getting well from a particular malady, our hope of reaching a final opinion must be seen as "a practical postulate" of inquiry that "does not go beyond the case actually in hand" (R958:198). As Peirce puts it elsewhere: "We must look forward to the explanation, not of all things, but of any given thing whatever" (W6:206).

The above notwithstanding, the claim that truth and final opinion are synonymous is a particularly strong one, and immediately raises two questions: Can we truly say that whatever we reach at this projected end of inquiry is true? And can there be truths that would not, or could not make it into a final opinion? In essence, both questions come down to the same. In admitting that for some questions a final opinion might still be false we are ipso facto admitting that for those questions the truth cannot be expressed in a final opinion. Hence, first we should tackle the second question, whether there could be any unknowable truths. Both questions, moreover, presuppose some independent notion of truth that is subsequently used as a benchmark. This can be another definition of truth, our conception of truth at the first grade of clearness, or something like our intuitions about truth. I will focus on the second, as the confidence with which we use a term in our daily lives not only inspires our definitions but also acts as the touchstone when seeking to identify where our intuitions lie.

I already touched upon the move toward a subjunctive conditional. On this interpretation inquiry need not be actually engaged in, nor need it be actually completed. All that is required is that *if* a question *were* to be looked into long enough by an indefinite community of inquirers, a final agreement about the answer *would* eventually be reached. But is this concession enough? There are certainly questions for which it is most unlikely, if not impossible, that a final opinion can ever be reached. What if we ask how often Cleopatra sneezed on her third birthday? This is certainly a well-formed question regarding a fairly well-defined empirical fact. However, as the historical record remains silent about it, the data required to answer it are no longer available (unless we allow for time travel or some farfetched form of determinism). Peirce calls such cases buried secrets (W3:274). If there are any such buried secrets, we can make assertions that may be true—like "Cleopatra sneezed twice on her third birthday"—that for contingent reasons cannot reach the status of a final opinion, so that the two concepts (truth and final opinion) cannot be said to be synonyms.

The general intuition behind this is that there is a fact of the matter—Cleopatra's sneezing twice—which is what it is irrespective of what we may think about anything, a fact that subsequently *could have become* an object of inquiry *had there been* people at the time that cared enough to do so. We can seek to capture this by formulating Peirce's conception of truth in terms of a counterfactual conditional. On this interpretation, the truth of an assertion is taken to be equivalent to the final opinion that would have been reached had the issue been inquired into when the relevant facts were still available. There certainly is something to be said for this, because whenever we claim that something happened, even though there was nobody there to perceive it, we are in effect tacitly projecting witnesses to it and proceed by implicitly describing what they would have perceived. Going this route will give us the following pragmatic definition of truth when applied to propositions:

> Proposition P is true if and only if, had all the facts necessary for establishing P been inquired into indefinitely by a sufficiently large community of investigators, this inquiry would have resulted in the permanently settled belief that P.

We can go a step further, however, and conjecture that there might be an alien species with sense organs so different from ours that their knowledge is wholly incommensurable with ours. This would allow them to know real truths about the world that would never enter any opinion of ours, final or otherwise. For this objection to work, the knowledge they gather must be so different from what we could learn, that in contrast to the blind and the deaf man mentioned before, no common ground can be reached as a potentially agreed upon explanation for the sensory impressions of both. It seems, though, that the postulate that there may be such alien truths fails to pass pragmatic muster. If these alien truths must be absolutely incognizable to us, then whether there are any such truths would have no conceivable practical consequences, so that the claim that there may be such truths is entirely without meaning (Section 7.3). Consequently, it cannot be raised as an objection. It would be like saying that transubstantiation is still possible even though the concept is wholly devoid of meaning (id.).

None of this is meant to deny that there are things "out there," things that are independent of what anyone may think about anything—independent even of whether there ever has, is, or will be any beings that perceive or think anything at all. All Peirce is saying is that when we claim that there are such things we must also admit that they can be known by us, at least in principle, because to do otherwise is to assert something without meaning. To the charge that this leads to anthropomorphism, Peirce responds by pointing out the foolishness of trying to escape it. As he explains in short article written for *The Open Court*: "Kant taught that our fundamental conceptions are merely the ineluctable ideas of a system of logical forms; nor is any occult transcendentalism requisite to show that this is so, and must be so. Nature only appears intelligible so far as it appears rational, that is, so far as its processes are seen to be like processes of thought" (CP3.422). Thus, for Peirce, we cannot have any idea that is not anthropomorphic (NEM4:313). I return to this in Section 9.5.

In sum, to the second question posed above—whether there can be any truths that would not, or could not make it into a final opinion—the answer is negative.

Turning now to the first question, can we say that any opinion held at the end of inquiry is true? Given what is said above, it is hard to conceive otherwise. What would a false final opinion be like? A false final opinion would say that things are otherwise than that they truly are. But given that everything must be at least in principle cognizable this can only mean that it is still possible that our opinion could be different, meaning that the opinion in question cannot be final. Consequently, no false opinion can be a final opinion.

Having settled that a final opinion cannot be false, can we say that this final opinion thus tells us the whole truth about its object? Peirce denies this. When discussing truth for Baldwin's *Dictionary*, he gives the example of a man who buys a horse, soon discovers that its hair had been dyed, and returns to the seller to complain that he was given a false representation. To this Peirce has the seller retort: "I never pretended to state every fact about the horse; what I said was true, so far as it professed to be true" (Baldwin 2:719). The point Peirce is driving at is that whereas truth is stated in propositional form—and is thus by its nature abstract—its object, reality, is not. Consequently, any true judgment about something real must be essentially unlike the object it is true of. As Peirce puts it, "its truth consists in the fact that it is impossible to correct it, and in the fact that it only professes to consider one aspect of the percept" (id.). Because of this, Peirce observes, "the perfect truth cannot be stated, except in the sense that it confesses its imperfection," adding that this confession "is an essential ingredient of truth" (id.).

8.3 Nominalism, realism, idealism

The above analysis of the pragmatic conceptions of truth and reality can be used to shed light on the issue of nominalism and realism, which is a recurrent theme in Peirce's thought. Because often realism is also contrasted with idealism, I also address how Peirce's realism relates to idealism.

In 1871, when reviewing Fraser's edition of Berkeley's *Works*, Peirce discovers that what fuels the debate between nominalists and realists is a different conception of reality. As it turns out, however, both can be seen as providing alternative interpretations of Scotus' definition on which something is real when it is independent of what you, or I, or anyone in particular may think it to be. For the nominalist, only the immediate outward constraints upon thought satisfy this definition. If reality is interpreted this way, then the nominalist's view that only particulars can be real follows naturally, as only what exerts pressure on our senses would be real. Consequently, for the nominalist, no laws or natural kinds can be real. They are merely the outcome of our attempts to make sense of the actual resistances we encounter.

The Peircean realist agrees with much of what the nominalist says. The realist too holds that the immediate outward constraints upon thought satisfy the definition, and the realist too acknowledges that natural laws and natural kinds are products of the mind. Where the realist disagrees is with the nominalist's insistence that no product of thought can ever be real. Now for the realist to be able to say this he must make a reasonable case that at least some products of thought satisfy Scotus' definition. Peirce's application of the pragmatic maxim to Scotus' definition, which I outlined above, is of great help here. It allows him to maintain that those products of our thought are real that would become the object of a final opinion. On this reading, a natural law would be real if at the end of inquiry it would be an object of a permanently settled belief. What this shows is that the nominalist's restriction of the real to outward constraints, or to particulars only, is too restrictive. Returning to the distinction between existence and reality drawn earlier, the nominalist is someone who holds that *only what exists* can be real. The realist, in contrast, holds that also those products of the mind are real that would become an object of a final opinion. Along the same lines, Peirce believes that there can be real possibilities, or as he also puts it, real can-bes, would-bes, could-have-beens, etc.

Although it is often presumed that science is nominalistic, Peirce argues that deep at heart science is realistic. Not only are scientists typically not interested in dead particulars—they are interested, rather, in laws or regularities—but without at least a tacit commitment to realism we cannot even have a coherent conception of science. It has been said that the success of modern science is because of its strong focus on facts rather than a priori theories that proclaim how things should be. Peirce does not disagree. What he disagrees with is that these facts must be particular. Take the experimental scientist. The experimental scientist interprets the meaning of an empirical statement as a prescription for an experiment that, if carried out correctly, will result in an experience of a given description (EP2:332). Now you might say that this confirms nominalism, as an experiment is always a particular operation upon a particular object leading to a particular result. However, to take such a position, Peirce counters, betrays a serious misunderstanding of what experiments are all about. The meaning of an experiment lies not in any of these particulars, nor in all of them together, but in the phenomenon that this particular event exemplifies, and that is not a particular at all:

> Indeed, it is not in an experiment, but in *experimental phenomena,* that rational meaning is said to consist. When an experimentalist speaks of a *phenomenon,* such as "Hall's phenomenon," "Zeemann's phenomenon" and its modification, "Michelson's phenomenon," or "the chessboard phenomenon," he does not mean any particular event that did happen to somebody in the dead past, but what *surely will* happen to everybody in the living future who shall fulfill certain conditions. (EP2:340)

Deep down, Peirce argues, the scientist must be a realist. He or she cannot be otherwise. Why experiment if all we get is a bunch of individual facts without any real connection between them. Though nominalism often appeals strongly to experimental scientists, its appeal is only superficial. To the seasoned experimentalist who comes to reflect upon the matter, nominalism quickly becomes a most implausible worldview. Peirce knows this from his own work doing experiments in geodetics:

> A pendulum . . . oscillates 86,400 times a day for twenty years, and every time with nearly the same period and nearly the same relative speeds during different aliquot parts of that period. Now, is there really any *law,* anything *general* operating in nature, or does the general character consist merely in our applying the same *name* to a number of instances which really have nothing in common? (R408:16)

Looked upon in such terms, nominalism quickly becomes a view that is very hard to maintain indeed. In sum, against the backdrop of Peirce's realism, the nominalist's restriction of the real to outward constraints (i.e. particulars) only—banishing all else to the realm of mere mental creations—not only shows itself to be unnecessarily restrictive but also makes science wholly inexplicable.

Now how about the relation between realism and idealism? Often these are considered opposites: The realist holds that our senses give us direct access to the external world, whereas the idealist argues that we can be aware only of our own ideas. Peirce, however, claims to be both at once. The key to understanding this lies again in his pragmatic understanding of Scotus' definition of reality. It allows him to say that although we can be aware only of our ideas, this is no impediment for their object to be real, while retaining a robust notion of an external world: "An Idealist need not deny the reality of the external world, any more than Berkeley did. For the reality of the external world *means* nothing except that real experience of duality" (CP5.539). Where Peirce differs from more traditional realists is that his is not a perceptual realism in which we are guaranteed a direct access to the external world through our senses. Peirce refers to his own view both as extreme scholastic realism and as conditional idealism, and at one point he states that it is merely Berkeleyanism with a few corrections (R322:22). One of these corrections, as we saw in Section 6.2, is that Peirce's idealism is an objective idealism, as it is grounded not in the individual but in the community.

CHAPTER NINE

Mind, God, and cosmos

In the previous chapter, we saw that metaphysics aims to provide a very general conception of the world wherein our specialized scientific endeavors can be grounded. We obtain such a conception by applying the findings of mathematics and the regulative laws of logic to the universe as it appears in philosophy—the latter being the study of what comes "within the range of every man's normal experience, and for the most part in every waking hour of his life" (CP1.241). Grounding metaphysics in logic also allows Peirce to "regard any metaphysics not based on pragmatism as a mere form of words to which no meaning whatever can be attached."[1] The discussion of truth and reality in the previous chapter clearly bears this out. In the current chapter, we look at physical and psychical metaphysics, which respectively study the most basic features of matter and mind. (Peirce also divides the special sciences into the physical sciences and the psychical sciences).

First we look at the issue of determinism, not only to introduce Peirce's tychism—the view that real chance is operative in the universe—but also to exemplify how, in Peirce's view, metaphysics depends upon mathematics. Next, I discuss the three modes of evolution that Peirce distinguishes, after which we move to his evolutionary cosmology. The latter half of the chapter is devoted to psychical metaphysics. We look at Peirce's evolutionary philosophy of mind and the related notion of concrete reasonableness, before concluding the chapter with a discussion of Peirce's conception of God and the relation between religion and science.

9.1 A critique of determinism

When constructing a general worldview, metaphysics relies not only on the more basic positive sciences but also on mathematics. In fact, it relies on the latter so heavily that Peirce repeatedly calls metaphysics the ape of mathematics. This means that when significant changes take place within mathematics (or, for that matter, in the more basic positive sciences), metaphysics should follow suit. Put briefly, it is an imperative of logic that metaphysicians should not tenaciously hold on to mathematical views after mathematicians have proven them wrong, not even if they lead to conclusions metaphysicians really like. A clear example is the case of determinism, or *necessitarianism* as it is also called in Peirce's time.

Around the middle of the nineteenth century it is discovered that the axioms of mathematics are not really axioms. Traditionally, axioms are taken to be propositions so undeniably true that any attempt to demonstrate them is less evident than the propositions themselves. An example of a mathematical axiom is the proposition that if two things are equal to a third they must also be equal to each other. Axioms feature prominently in Euclid's *Elements,* a work that was the standard mathematics textbook for over two millennia. Euclid called them *common notions,* things we all believe to be true. Over time these common notions morphed into things we cannot but believe to be true, because they are self-evident. What happens mid-nineteenth century is that some of these "things we cannot but believe to be true" are shown to be false, whereas others are shown to be far from self-evident. One of the main engines behind this is the discovery of non-Euclidean geometries. Traditionally, it was believed that physical space had to be Euclidean—that is, conformant to Euclid's axioms. Space clearly looks Euclidean, which is also to be expected as it is our experience of handling the ruler and compass in physical space that inspired the axioms to begin with. Now when we construe a triangle through a point on earth and the centers of the Sun and Mars, and subsequently calculate the angles, we find their sum to be sufficiently close to 180° to attribute any differences to errors in observation or measurement. Hence, despite discrepancies between what the theory prescribes and what observation reveals, mathematicians long maintained that physical space is Euclidean by raising it to the level of a norm; that is to say, by making the theory say what value our measurements should aspire to, or what the value would be under ideal (i.e. error free) rather than actual circumstances. This they could do because, in their view, Euclidian space followed indisputably from self-evident axioms, so that we cannot even think space to be otherwise.

This traditional view is refuted during Peirce's life when it is discovered that one can develop consistent geometries that are not Euclidean. This means that we *can* think space to be other than Euclidian. Rather than joining the long list of people who tried to prove Euclid's parallel postulate, mathematicians like Bolyai, Lobachevski, and Riemann examined what happens when we reject the postulate outright, and they found that they could create consistent alternative geometries in which space is curved. In fact, it proved possible to form an infinite number of geometries, each with a differently curved space. One characteristic of a curved space is that the angles of a triangle *do not* add up to 180°. In fact, Euclidian space, which is now one among infinite alternatives, is the *only* space where the three angles add up to exactly 180°.

Where does this leave the old notion that physical space is Euclidian? There is, Peirce argues, no evidence for this at all. Quite the opposite, it is far more likely that physical space is *almost but not quite* Euclidian—that is to say, its curvature must be small enough to be accounted for by the same observations that make people think space is Euclidean. The argument runs as follows: Given any set of actual measurements there is no reason at all to assume that the sum of the angles must be exactly 180° rather than any of the infinite values that are extremely close to it. To be more precise, the odds are infinity to one that it is not. In sum, with the advent of non-Euclidian geometries, and the accompanying rejection of mathematical axioms as self-evident truths about the physical universe, any geometry of physical space will be a purely empirical affair. The way mathematicians have responded to this is by turning away from the actual world and making their discipline a purely hypothetical science. This shift, or at least Peirce's reading of it, is described in Section 2.2.

How does this all affect metaphysics? If mathematics has to let go of axioms as self-evident truths about the world, then metaphysicians can no longer rely on them either. Moreover, whereas mathematicians can change their game by no longer talking about the actual world, metaphysicians, whose task it is to provide a general description of that world, do not have that option. In short, metaphysicians can no longer rely on mathematics-style axioms.

A popular metaphysical doctrine that Peirce believes is no longer tenable is determinism, which is the view that whatever happens is always precisely determined by antecedent causes, or precisely determined by law. It is clear, Peirce observes, that such a view "cannot be rendered probable by observation" because when we try to verify any law "we find discrepancies between observation and theory, which we rightly set down as errors of observation" (W8:89). The determinist's response is that his view does not rely at all on empirical evidence. The determinist regards it instead as a metaphysical axiom—a truth about the world that is so evident that any attempt to prove it will be less evident than that truth itself, and ipso facto a truth that no empirical results can ever discredit. However, with the idea of mathematical axioms blown out of the water, and determinism being, essentially, a product of analytical mechanics— which is a mathematical theory—the determinist's axiom becomes a mere article of faith. And just as we can say that it is far more likely that the sum of the angles of any triangle in physical space is almost but not exactly 180°, it is far more likely that whatever happens is not exactly determined by laws or by antecedent causes either, even if it is very nearly so. Here too, any deviations must be so small as to be obscured by the unavoidable errors of observation. Although in the strictest sense determinism is still possible as an explanatory hypothesis about how the world works, it is a very unlikely hypothesis and one that is grounded entirely in an article of faith that is but the hollow echo of exploded self-evident truths. Hence, the determinist hypothesis is to be rejected. Instead, the most likely position to take is that even the most engrained physical laws are not completely deterministic, but that there are sporadic, infinitesimal violations that may form the seeds of new possibilities, or further growth. Peirce thereby shows that the view, popular in his time as well as ours, that chance is a purely epistemic notion (so that attributing anything to chance is only a confession of our ignorance) is unfounded. Infinity to one there is real chance in the world.

9.2 Three modes of evolution

The previous section shows what scientific metaphysics looks like for Peirce: it is the application of the findings of mathematics, phaneroscopy, and the normative sciences to the everyday facts of life without any predetermined opinions about what the answers should be. Before delving into Peirce's cosmology, it is helpful to first see what in Peirce's eyes requires explanation. Clearly not everything demands an explanation. If Junhee in Korea happens to raise her eyebrows shortly after Olivia sneezes in the United States, we have two facts without any definite relationship between them. Consequently, we cannot in any real sense *explain* how the two relate. The situation is different when Olivia sneezes incessantly every time she enters a used bookstore. Here there is enough of a connection to make us suspect that there might be a definite relation that can be captured in an explanation—for example, an abundance of dust mites in the store causes an allergic reaction that manifests itself in frequent sneezing. Now, an explanation brings together three things: the thing to be explained, that in terms of which it is explained, and the terms that connect the two. Consequently, we cannot give an explanation of a pure first, as in the process we would obliterate it by embedding it in a definite relation with a second (as a result of which it is no longer a pure first). Similarly, we cannot explain a pure second, as we would still be inserting a definite relation between things where previously there was only brute or blind (i.e. inexplicable) opposition. In both cases, rather than explaining something, we are replacing it with something altogether different. An explanation becomes *possible* only when there is a definite relation between things, that is, where there is thirdness. An explanation is moreover *required,* Peirce argues, whenever we posit or deliberatively rely on a definite relation. That is to say, it is an imperative of logic that we may not rely on or posit a definite relation and then call this relation absolutely inexplicable. For the metaphysician this means that laws cannot be primitive facts—that is, facts not requiring an explanation.

Recapitulating, we can say that there is real chance in the world, that pure chance, being a first, requires no explanation, and that natural laws do require an explanation. Combining these three elements provides Peirce with a strategy for explaining natural laws: our task becomes that of showing how natural laws could have evolved from chance. Peirce follows this strategy in his cosmology, which thereby provides the explanation for the occurrence of natural laws as well as their overall nature. It is subsequently up to the special sciences to determine what these natural laws are. The idea that laws evolve brings in the notion of evolution, so that Peirce's cosmology is an evolutionary cosmology.

Rather than affiliating himself with existing evolutionary theories as they developed within the special sciences, Peirce grasps back to phaneroscopy and the normative sciences for the materials from which to develop a truly metaphysical conception of evolution. In agreement with his doctrine of the categories he distinguishes three modes of evolution. Before discussing them a few things may be observed. First, since all objects of knowledge involve all three of the categories, any theory of evolution must involve elements of all three as well, no matter how faintly. Second, true to his refutation of nominalism, the types of evolution Peirce distinguishes are all realistic. Third, since the objective of a theory of evolution is to explain how things evolve, thirdness will be a key element in any theory of evolution. However, as we saw in Section 3.2, Peirce also distinguishes, besides genuine thirdness, two types of degenerate thirdness. This pattern returns here as well and accordingly Peirce distinguishes three modes of evolution, one genuine and two degenerate.

The first mode of evolution is Darwinian. Evolution occurs due to small, accidental variations in the process of reproduction. As these variations are wholly products of chance—which is what it is independently of anything else—this type of evolution is due to firstness being operative in nature. Utilizing the Greek word for chance Peirce calls this first mode of evolution *tychastic evolution,* or *tychasm,* and the view that real chance is operative in nature *tychism* (W8:194). No evolution, however, can be a product of chance alone, as it would be mere change without direction. A second force is needed to provide direction. This Darwinians find in the struggle for existence (W8:102). This struggle for existence requires that there is something to struggle with—that is, a second—and this introduces the element of secondness. The resultant evolution, as a determinate relation, brings in the element of thirdness. Peirce considers this a degenerate type of evolution because it is driven by chance, or firstness, and not by law, or thirdness.

In the second mode, evolution is caused by the blind impact of outward forces. For instance, according to Clarence King, an American geologist and personal acquaintance of Peirce, evolution occurs when sudden and dramatic changes in the environment disrupt existing habits or patterns.[2] Because it is merely the blind impact of outward forces that causes the change, secondness is the key operative principle in this mode of evolution. This type of evolution is deterministic, as wherever it is not we would have to default to tychism for our explanation. In agreement with this, Peirce names this second mode of evolution *anancastic*—after Ananke, the Greek goddess of necessity—reserving *anancism* for the view that evolution works this way (W8:194). The great success of analytical mechanics in modern times proved a strong impetus for deterministic thinking (Section 9.1), making anancism a preferred view for looking at the evolution of living as well as nonliving things. Besides King, Peirce also cites Herbert Spencer and August Weissman as proponents of this view. Like tychasm also anancasm is a degenerative type of evolution. Peirce distinguishes two types of anancastic evolution, one where the force is inward and one where the force is outward. As will be shown in the next section, Peirce rejects anancism on the ground that a deterministic mechanical principle cannot spawn diversity. In Peirce's eyes this is fatal because a key premise of any theory of evolution is that "things must on the whole have proceeded from the Homogeneous to the Heterogeneous" (W4:548).

Neither mode of evolution evolves according to a plan or purpose or inward striving. Neither is directed by law, rather law is a by-product that remains itself without efficacy. This is different with the third mode Peirce distinguishes and for which he sees Lamarck as a precursor. Here evolution takes place through habit formation and transmission. This cannot be explained, Peirce argues, in terms of mere chance or blind mechanical cause, but requires some sort of mediation. The sort of mediation Peirce has in mind here is best exemplified in what he calls "the law of mind" (W8:135ff). Ideas or mental states affect one another and become welded together in a process that is neither necessary nor invariable. According to Peirce, the law of mind only exerts a weak, or gentle force; it is a force that renders certain things more likely than they would be had there been no such law. And this weakness is no defect of the law. On the contrary, without it the law would not be able to produce anything new and could not really be an evolutionary law. Consequently, rather than speaking of evolution being subject to laws, Peirce prefers to speak of evolution being subject to habits. Since habits are generals, this third mode of evolution is a product of thirdness being operative in nature.

Peirce calls this third and highest mode of evolution, evolution by creative love, or *agapasm,* and he calls the view that the law of love is really operative in nature *agapism* (W8:194). The notion of love as a cosmic principle is not new. In ancient Greece, Empedocles distinguished besides the four elements (earth, water, fire, and air) two cosmic principles: love and hate (W8:184). The first is the force that brings elements together; the second is the force that separates them. The two principles let Empedocles explain creation and destruction, life and death, etc. Peirce rejects Empedocles' love-hate dichotomy, following instead the Christian doctrine that states that just as darkness is an absence of light, hate is an imperfect state of love (id.). Consequently, for Peirce, love is both the force that unites and the force that divides. By choosing a single principle rather than a dichotomy of opposing principles, Peirce's interpretation of love is true to his regulative principle of synechism (Section 4.3).

Peirce describes this third mode of evolution as follows:

> The agapastic development of thought is the adoption of certain mental tendencies, not altogether heedlessly, as in tychasm, nor quite blindly by the mere force of circumstances or of logic, as in anancasm, but by an immediate attraction for the idea itself, whose nature is divined before the mind possesses it, by the power of sympathy, that is, by virtue of the continuity of mind. (W8:196)

In sum, Peirce distinguishes three modes of evolution depending on whether evolution is a product of firstness (absolute chance), secondness (inward or outward necessity), or thirdness (habit). Our next task is to utilize these to explain the origin and nature of natural laws. This brings us to Peirce's evolutionary cosmology.

9.3 The origin and nature of natural laws

The aim of metaphysics is to furnish us with a *Weltanschauung* that can form a basis for the special sciences. Part of what we must expect from such a *Weltanschauung* is an account of natural laws, as it is a basic presupposition of the special sciences that there are such laws (Section 8.3). Peirce believes that his evolutionary cosmology can provide us with such an explanation.

The evolution of the cosmos, Peirce argues, is *hyperbolic*, it "proceeds from one state of things in the infinite past, to a different state of things in the infinite future" (W8:386).[3] The beginning state is one of pure possibility; the end state is one of a "complete triumph of law and absence of all spontaneity" (id.). That Peirce situates the end-points in the infinite past and the infinite future can be taken as a hypothesis that is dictated by his synechism, or the doctrine of continuity. To say otherwise and stipulate that there must have been somehow an absolute beginning (or an absolute end) posits a radical discontinuity for which there is no ground.

Earlier, when discussing Peirce's criticism of determinism, we saw that he made heavy use of the mathematical notion of the infinite. According to Peirce, we can never say that natural phenomena obey laws with absolute precision because in each and every case an infinite number of infinitesimal departures make it more likely that laws are closely obeyed rather than that they are perfectly obeyed. In his evolutionary cosmology, Peirce makes again extensive use of the mathematical notion of the infinite, drawing a distinction between the infinitely distant past, and a very, very distant past (W8:387).

Peirce describes the infinitely distant past in terms of pure possibility. It is the universe as a pure first; there is nothing to which it is second. This implies that its own composition may not be such that it can be second to any of its parts (like when we are second to our own body in the experience of a belly ache). This requires that at this stage the universe is wholly unstructured and wholly without regularity. Such a universe cannot (yet) exist, nor can anything (yet) exist in it. This because to say that something exists means to say that it stands out and interacts with other things like it in a persistent manner, and this demands not only secondness, but also at least some level of regularity.

This primordial state cannot be described, because, as we saw (Section 3.2), a pure first cannot be described without distorting it to such a degree that it no longer is a first. For the same reason, we can neither give nor demand an explanation for it. But we can say some things about it. In this chaos of possibility, bits of similitude may appear and be swallowed up again, and we can say that in the infinitely long run they will appear. For the same reason such bits will reappear, and there will emerge a slight tendency to habituation. The latter Peirce derives from the doctrine of chances, which shows that over the long run chance has a concentrative effect (W4:551). In this way, firstness gives rise to secondness, and secondness gives rise to thirdness. To put it briefly, Peirce sees the universe as a self-enveloping whole that in its higher stages increasingly develops through self-control: "The tendency to form habits or tendency to generalize, is something which grows by its own action, by the habit of taking habits itself growing. Its first germs arose from pure chance. There were slight tendencies to obey rules that had been followed, and these tendencies were rules which were more and more obeyed by their own action" (CP8.317). Physical laws thus develop in a process not unlike how a stream of water wears a bed for itself (CP5.492).

Within this process, the universe loses in potentiality and gains in determinateness. Laws emerge more or less like habits. Only after the establishment of habits can things come into existence, as an existing thing is nothing but something that stands in a certain habitual relation to other things that are sufficiently like it. Similarly time, as a determinate relation between events, emerges as a product of habit formation. Just as we cannot say that in its very early stages the universe (or anything in it) exists, so we cannot say that any of these early events take place in time. Existence, time, and for that matter space, are all relatively late products of the cosmic evolution. The distinction between the infinitely distant past and the very, very distant past may be of help here. If the origin of the universe is situated in the infinite past, then no matter how long we go back in time we will always reach a point that is still infinitely far removed from the origin of the universe. What is more, we will always reach a point where evolution has already been going on for an infinitely long time (W8:387). Put differently, if the universe originated infinitely long ago, then our concept of time is not applicable to the whole past, but only to the denumerable past.

Peirce associates the potentiality, freedom, chance, or spontaneity that self-develops into habits, with mind, or spirit: "Everything is of the nature of mind,—even material phenomena," Peirce writes, adding that, "mind is not necessarily person. Rather, a person is mind whose parts are coordinated in a particular way" (W6:439). Thus, in contrast to the materialists, who hold that everything in the universe is made of dead matter, and to whom the human mind is nothing but a very intricate piece of that matter that somehow "came to life," Peirce maintains that living mind is the primeval constituent of the universe, and that matter is nothing but mind that has been deadened almost completely by habit. As Peirce puts it in "The Architecture of Theories": "The one intelligible theory of the universe is that of objective idealism, that matter is effete mind, inveterate habits becoming physical laws" (W8:106). Hence, true to his doctrine of continuity, Peirce holds that there is no substantive difference between the human mind and a stone; they differ only in the manner and the degree in which they are bound by habit.

To illustrate that his evolutionary cosmology can account for natural laws, Peirce shows how Newton's famous inverse square law could be explained as a product of chance and habit formation. On Newton's law the strength with which two bodies attract one another is inversely proportional to the square of their distance. The law of chance, Peirce argues, shows us that bodies that repel or do not attract will in the long run "get thrown out of the region of space leaving the mutually attracting bodies" (W4:553). For the remaining bodies, the relation expressed in Newton's law may only be the average, with matter that attracts inversely to a higher power of the distance tending to clump together, and matter that attracts inversely to a lower power also floating away over time (id.). The type of laws that thus ensue are statistical laws (W4:551), making Peirce an early proponent of statistical mechanics.

9.4 Mind, self, and person

Most evolutionary theories hold that at critical junctions phenomena such as life, consciousness, mind, and self-awareness emerge as new properties of matter. Peirce, as we have seen, takes the opposite course. Rather than taking matter as primordial and mind a modification of it, he takes mind as primordial and holds that matter is a modification of mind. This objective idealism, as Peirce calls it, commits him to say that "the laws of physics are the same as those of mental representations" (CD:2974). The difference between mind and matter is only the degree to which they are fixed by habits.

When discussing the human mind, Peirce takes an externalist view. He denies that we somehow have a direct and full access to our minds, as is supposed, for instance, by the Cartesians. In his *Journal of Speculative Philosophy* series, Peirce shows that we have no intuitive knowledge and no faculty of introspection, but that we gain all our knowledge from observation—and this he takes to apply also to any knowledge we have of our own mind. So, what do we perceive when we observe what we call our mind? Some would say consciousness. Peirce rejects this idea. One reason is Eduard Hartmann's discovery that we have also unconscious mind, so that "consciousness is a special, and not a universal accompaniment of mind" (CP7.366). But that's not all. When psychologists talk about consciousness, Peirce observes, what they really talk about is feeling. Now feeling, Peirce claims, is a simple quality. What constitutes mind, he argues, is not simple feeling or consciousness per se, but the establishment of connections between feelings, that is, of habits. In this process, feeling loses in intensity. "The development of the human mind," Peirce explains, "has practically extinguished all feelings, except a few sporadic kinds, sounds, colours, smells, warmth, etc." (W8:147). That is to say, rather than being the expression of feeling, thought involves the extinction of feeling. Peirce does not deny that consciousness, or feeling, features in a typical explanation of how thoughts come about, but its role is not categorically different from other factors that are crucial to a thought's creation. Peirce gives as an example his inkstand. If it runs out of ink, he writes, my thoughts cease to flow as well (CP7.366). In light of all of this Peirce concludes that psychologists are mistaken when they say that to understand thought we must study consciousness. Not without sarcasm he even adds that this view is about as bizarre as where an ichthyologist to define his science as a study of water (CP7.368).

Faithful to his doctrine of the categories, Peirce argues that three elements are operative in our mind, feeling being only one of them. Besides feeling we experience brute opposition, "as when a person blindfold runs against a post," which is an experience no analysis can reduce to a mere feeling (W8:96). And, third, there are situations where connections between feelings are determined by a general rule, or governed by habit, either consciously or unconsciously (W8:97).

What strikes Peirce as most important when reflecting upon the mind is not consciousness, or feeling, but the presence of an inner dialog. We are constantly talking to ourselves. This causes Peirce to conclude that what we call our thought is a derivative of our communication with others, a view that is confirmed by the fact that small children converse with others before conversing with themselves. A subsequent suppression of the use of the lips and vocal cords makes this conversation private; that is to say, only we can "hear" ourselves think. Because in speech we apply general terms to particulars, speech involves the establishment of habits. For instance, when expressing our aches and pains in language we reduce an infinite variety of bodily discomforts to a fairly small set of expressions, such as "it hurts," "I'm nauseous," or "there is a tension in my shoulders," and we subsequently interpret the former in terms of the latter.

A consequence of Peirce's dialogic interpretation of mind is that it does not develop, so to speak, from the inside out, as with Descartes, but from the outside in. Through our conversations with others, and our interaction with the environment more broadly, we come to realize that what others say may be a better guide to what is going on than our sensory experience. Peirce gives the example of a mother warning her child that the stove is hot. The child—whose conception of what is hot or cold is still confined to what it actually touches—disbelieves what he hears, as the stove does not feel hot to him. It is only by ignoring the warning and touching the stove that the child discovers that his mother's testimony was a better sign of truth than his own experience. In this way, Peirce argues, the child "becomes aware of ignorance and it is necessary to suppose a *self* in which this ignorance can inhere" (W2:202). This self is thus literally a hypothesis raised by the individual to account for the experience of error and ignorance, and this hypothesis is a product of the individual's communication with others.

In his *Journal of Speculative Philosophy* series Peirce also defends the claim that we only think in signs (W2:207). That every thought is a sign means, given Peirce's triadic conception of signs, that every thought connects three elements: a representamen, an object, and an interpretant (Section 5.2). It also means that thought should be understood as a process of semeiosis, as a dynamic and continuous process of sign action in which each sign gives rise to an interpretant, which in turn becomes a sign that gives rise to *its* interpretant, and so on. Peirce then argues that every modification of consciousness is an inference. On the traditional Cartesian view, the mind is filled with private thoughts. Only when we want to communicate any of these we must translate them into public signs, such as words, symphonies, or paintings.[4] By claiming that we always think in signs, Peirce puts this Cartesian view on its head. Thought is not something private, hidden from all the rest of the world, but is inherently public. Thought does not reside within so-called individual minds, but resides in the public sign structure through which we communicate. It is only *internalized* when the interior dialog we call the human mind becomes the sign's vehicle, as opposed to some publicly accessible object like a sound wave, painting, or book. Using an analogy with physics, Peirce observes that "just as we say that a body is in motion and not that motion is in a body we ought to say that we are in thought and not that thoughts are in us" (W2:227). Based on considerations like these, Peirce identifies a second and related mistake prevalent among psychologists (the first being the identification of mind with consciousness), namely the propensity to situate the mind in the brain (CP7.366).

If we only think in signs, then we also appear to ourselves also as a sign. What is more, given the pragmatic maxim, the conception we have of ourselves cannot be anything other than the effects we might conceive ourself to have. Since each of these effects is a sign, man is nothing but a sign to himself and others. Taking language in its widest sense (i.e. including gestures, tattoos, paintings, songs, etc.), Peirce concludes that "my language is the sum total of myself; for the man is the thought" (W2:241). Peirce even goes so far as to claim that there is no significant difference between a person and a word. Granted, the man-sign is far more complex than the word-sign, and the sign vehicles are different, but these differences are only relative. As Peirce formulates it: "The word or sign which man uses *is* the man himself. For, as the fact that every thought is a sign, taken in conjunction with the fact that life is a train of thought, proves that man is a sign; so, that every thought is an *external* sign, proves that man is an external sign" (W2:241). A major obstacle to seeing ourselves this way, Peirce writes, is our tendency to identify ourselves with our will, meaning our ability to control the animal organism that accompanies our self. However, by itself this is only a brute force; it is blind. What constitutes our identity is not the brute force we can exert on our bodies or on our bodily desires, but the *consistency* we acquire in what we do and think (id.). This brings us to the notion of personal identity.

Personal identity, or personhood, Peirce argues, is a kind of coordination or connection between ideas (CP6.228). As the occurrence of multiple personality disorder shows, the unity of personhood is not the simple product of a unique relationship to a particular human body, brain, or consciousness. It is a product of consistency in thought. Personhood may reside in an individual, as it typically does, but this is by no means necessary. Also a well-functioning team may be considered a person; it may even act like a single body. A jockey with his horse may be considered a person. We may even call Peirce and his inkwell a person (remember that his thoughts stopped flowing when his ink ran out?). Examples like these undermine traditional notions of personhood and individual mind. In fact, Peirce considers the idea of personal identity—that is, of an autonomous mind that we can call ours—"the vulgarest delusion of vanity," writing that "your neighbors are, in a measure, yourself and in far greater measure than, without deep studies in psychology, you would believe" (EP2:2). Elsewhere, he gives the following analogy to counter the popular notion of an independent and self-reliant individual who enters society only to further his private interests: "A *person* is in truth like a cluster of stars, which appears to be *one* star when viewed with the naked eye, but which scanned with the telescope of scientific psychology is found on the one hand to be multiple within itself, and on the other hand to have no absolute demarcation from a neighboring condensation" (R403:2f)—the closer we get to it the more it dissolves before our eyes. We speak proudly of *our* mind, but, Peirce observes, in truth "it is we who float upon its surface and belong to it more than it belongs to us" (CP7.558). It is not we who think, but it is thought that develops through us. When we have difficulty expressing "our thoughts" it is not because they are somehow superior to the crude medium in which we try to express them, but because they are yet not fully developed in us.

9.5 The development of concrete reasonableness

The idea that the universe somehow exhibits reason is about as old as philosophy itself. In fact, people have been so impressed by the reasonableness of the universe that it led to the view that it must have been designed by an intelligence far superior to us. Though this argument goes back at least to Socrates,[5] William Paley expresses it most forcibly in his *Natural Theology*. Meticulously comparing the eye with a telescope Paley argues that the "contrivances of nature" far surpass the contrivances of men, not only in their complexity, but also in their variety.[6] From this Paley concludes that just as telescopes are products of design, so must be eyes, and that the complexity and variety of the latter points conclusively to God as the Great Designer of the universe and all that's in it. Hence, for Paley, the universe is reasonable because an infinitely intelligent God designed it as such. Paley, however, explicitly presupposes the (pre)existence of natural laws, arguing that it is the knowledge of these laws that enabled God to design eyes and man to design telescopes.

For Peirce, this once again puts the cart before the horse. Rather than conjecturing that reason somehow exists independently of the universe, and that the universe is subsequently shaped in its image, Peirce argues that the reasonableness of the universe is a natural product of evolution itself. That is to say, without any preset plan or external supervision, the universe taken by itself in its evolutionary development becomes more and more guided by what we call reason. Since we too emerge within that universe, Peirce can maintain that this reason not only governs the outer world we call nature but also the inner world (or, better put, the interior dialog) that we call our mind. Briefly put, we are endowed with reason because the world is. And because the reason or reasonableness we call ours reflects the reasonableness of the world, we are able to use our reason to understand the world, that is, to reduce the manifold of appearances to the unity of law. As Peirce explains: "if the universe conforms, with any approach to accuracy, to certain highly pervasive laws, and if man's mind has been developed under the influence of those laws, it is to be expected that he should have a *natural light,* or *light of nature,* or *instinctive insight,* or genius, tending to make him guess those laws aright, or nearly aright" (CP5.604).

Peirce uses the phrase *concrete reasonableness,* rather than reasonableness or reason per se, because "reason" is a general term and general terms are always open-ended. They can never be completely embodied. As Peirce explains: "The most insignificant of general ideas always involves conditional predictions or requires for its fulfilment that events should come to pass, and all that ever can have come to pass must fall short of completely fulfilling its requirements ... [so that] the development of Reason requires as a part of it the occurrence of more individual events than ever can occur" (EP2:254f). This causes Peirce to conclude that reason "always must be in a state of incipiency, of growth" (EP2:255).

Concrete reasonableness is reason insofar as it is actually embodied within the universe.

Without there being in nature itself "an element of Reasonableness to which we can train our own reason to conform more and more [recall that Peirce defines the self in terms of ignorance and error] there could be no such thing as logical goodness or badness," and logic as a normative enterprise would not be applicable (CP5.160). The above account further confirms the regulative principle that we should have ourselves be guided by the hope that we can make our own reason conform to the reason imbedded in the universe—even if only in the long run—as in such hope, Peirce explains, "lies the only possibility of any knowledge" (id.). Connecting inquiry to the development of reasonableness in the cosmos further allows Peirce to deny that reason has only instrumental value—that it is merely a useful tool for helping us to get what we want—and argue instead that the pursuit of reason is an end in itself. He even identifies it as the highest good, or *summum bonum*. As Peirce explains: "Under this conception, the ideal of conduct will be to execute our little function in the operation of the creation by giving a hand toward rendering the world more reasonable whenever, as the slang is, it is 'up to us' to do so" (EP2:255).

Peirce's notion of concrete reasonableness ties in with that of critical common-sensism (Chapter 6). The critical common-sensist, if he is a good pragmatist adores not doubt, but power, "not the sham power of brute force, which, even in its own specialty of spoiling things, secures but slight results; but the creative power of reasonableness, which subdues all other powers, and rules over them with its sceptre, knowledge, and its globe, love" (CP5.520).

9.6 God, science, and religion

Though Peirce rejects the Kantian notion of metaphysics as the study of God, freedom, and immortality, opting instead for an overtly scientific metaphysics that is aimed at providing a *Weltanschauung* wherein the sciences can be grounded, a few lines should be devoted to Peirce's notion of God and the relation between science and religion. Especially because of the work of Darwin, the relation between science and religion was hotly debated in the second half of the nineteenth century.

When discussing God and religion, Peirce is not addressing the religious person, as if the latter would need a philosophy of religion to ground his religiosity. That would be like "inviting a man to see the body of his wife dissected" with the aim of giving him a better understanding of the object of his love (CP8.125). Instead, Peirce directs himself against those who make factual claims about God—typically with an air of infallibility—and he does so mostly with the aim of examining what we can truly say about God, and whether a belief in God, or a religious life more generally, can be reconciled with a scientific life. Peirce sees that theologians in particular make many claims about God that are antithetical to science. In fact, theologians are, in Peirce's view, a prime example of sham reasoners—people who already know what their conclusion should be, and then look for ways to support it. This type of reasoning goes straight against all Peirce stands for with his conception of logic as a normative science and his insistence on the scientific attitude. As he writes to the American psychologist James McKeen Cattell: "The majority don't care so much for truth. What they care for is to see that poor God doesn't get injured."[7] In contrast to the sham reasoning of theologians, Peirce firmly believes that if there is a God, inquiry that is engaged in with the scientific attitude will, in the long run, reveal all we can say about Him. Hence, Peirce's intended audience is not the religious man, but the men of science.

Peirce's evolutionary cosmology described above, which is idealistic in that mind is the primordial substance, allows for various conceptions of God. God can still be conceived as the Creator of the universe. But if so, this God would have to be very different from Paley's notion of a Great Designer. Taking the view that we are created in the image of God, theologians often see the mind of God as the perfection of our own mind, as it is our mind that distinguishes us from the brutes. The conception of God as all-powerful, omniscient, and entirely good is a good example. It picks up certain traits of our minds and pushes them to perfection. Peirce sees this view as ludicrous at best. As he complains to the theologian, "all you know of 'minds' is from the actions of animals with brains or ganglia like yourselves, or at furthest like a cockroach. To apply such a word to *God* is precisely like the old pictures which show him like an aged man leaning over to look out from above a cloud" (CP6.199). When taken literally, it's false; when taken figuratively, though strictly not false, it's ludicrous. On Peirce's evolutionary cosmology—where the universe is the effect of pure potentiality, or feeling—God's mind would have to be characterized as pure potentiality and feeling. Not only would there be nothing existing, but there would be no generality, hence no ideas, and no rationality. Because an event that occurs by absolute chance introduces something new, it can be considered a creative act,[8] so that such a non-existing, unreal, and perfectly vacuous God can still be considered a Creator.

An alternative approach is to say that this God develops, or grows, with His creation. This gives us at least two options. One is that God remains external to His creation, which leaves us with an awkward dichotomy. Peirce rejects this option. If the universe is what emerges from pure chance, and God is not part of it, then God *ipso facto* cannot be real (R683:26). This is pragmatism at work. A second option is to say that God should be identified with the developing concrete reasonableness of the universe. This second option could be cast as a double-aspect theory, with science and religion representing two sides of the same coin. The *world-process*, as Peirce calls it, when examined from the aspect of nature can be conceived in terms of development and growth (this is the cosmology discussed above), or when examined from the aspect of God, in terms of manifestation and creation. God then reveals Himself to us insofar as we comprehend the concrete reasonableness of the cosmos. Peirce's conception of personhood outlined above further allows him to say that God is a person (CP6.157).

The above account further allows Peirce to say that in genuine inquiry—inquiry aimed at truly finding out how things are without any sort of axe to grind—"man, with all his miserable littleness, becomes gradually more and more imbued with the Spirit of God" (CP5.402n2). Peirce there leaves us with a conception of God that is "the highest flight toward an understanding of the original of the whole physico-psychical universe that we can make," and he adds that this "has the advantage over the agnostics and other views of offering to our apprehension an object to be loved." (R1334:23). Hence, for Peirce, there is no real difference between religion and science. It is rather the outdated creeds of existing religions, dogmatically clung to, that cause a rift between science and religion.

In 1909, Peirce writes to William James that, even though his cosmological papers make a strong argument for a deity, a still better argument is found in his 1908 "A Neglected Argument for the Reality of God."[9]

Defining God as the necessary being that is the creator of all we experience, Peirce first distinguishes argument from argumentation. By *argument* he means "any process of thought reasonably tending to produce a definite belief"; by *argumentation* he means "an Argument proceeding upon definitely formulated premises" (EP2:435). Thomas Aquinas's famous five ways of proving the existence of God are clear examples of argumentations.[10] For Aquinas, the existence of God follows deductively from carefully crafted sets of premises that unbelievers are presumed to accept, and the argumentations are primarily intended to counter other argumentations that argue for the contrary. The result is a largely academic exercise that has little bearing upon the common believer. Peirce's neglected argument is not at all like this. It is an *argument* for God, without being an argumentation. Whereas an argumentation combines carefully crafted premises such that they lead to, or even necessitate, the conclusion, Peirce's neglected argument has no clearly identifiable premises, nor a clearly identifiable form, while still necessitating the conclusion.

Peirce's neglected argument originates in what he terms *musement*, a state of mind in which we let our thoughts float freely without purpose. Taking his cues from Friedrich Schiller's notion of *Spiel-Trieb*, Peirce sees this musement as pure play—a playful dialog with oneself that is wholly free of any rules or strictures and serves no purpose but its agreeable effect upon the muser. According to Peirce, such free and playful contemplation of the universe, the nature of which is inescapably awe-inspiring, inevitably leads to the hypothesis, however lightly entertained, of a God. Peirce then continues by stating that once the hypothesis is entertained, the muser "will, as a fact, find himself utterly incapable of doubting it, which is more than a *Proof* of it to him,—it is a *Rational Compulsion*" (R641:21). One way of casting this is that musement leads to an *instinctive* belief in God. That is to say, the rational compulsion Peirce talks about does not have its origin in logic—conceived as conscious, self-controlled reasoning—but in the muser's semi- or perhaps even wholly unconscious *logica utens* (Section 3.2) that reflects the reasonableness of the cosmos (Section 9.5).

In Peirce's view, the neglected argument is reasonable because, "it naturally results in the most intense and living determination (*Bestimmung*) of the soul toward shaping the Muser's whole conduct into conformity with the hypothesis that God is Real and very near;

and such a determination of the soul in regard to any proposition is the very Essence of a living Belief in such a proposition" (EP2:446). This goes back to Peirce's pragmatism, on which the meaning of a concept is exhausted by the habits, or dispositions, to which it gives rise (Section 7.1).

In contrast to traditional argumentations for God, the most solid form of the neglected argument—which Peirce calls *the humble argument*—does not come from the learned theologian, but comes from the uninformed lay believer. It is the kind of argument that is so strongly dependent upon seeing things as they are, that one's existing beliefs are an impediment rather than of help. The situation here is not all that different from the artist who, having been taught that snow is white, must first return to a state of innocence that allows him to learn its true color (Section 3.1). In both cases, we can say that "the facts that stand before our face and eyes and stare us in the face are far from being, in all cases, the ones most easily discerned" (W8:156f). From this perspective, we may even say that much unbelief in God is a product of organized religions and their creeds, as they divert us away from truths that would otherwise be perceived more easily. It is equally, though, a product of the metaphysical doctrine of nominalism, which prematurely, and falsely, reduces all that is real to brute existence (Section 8.3).

A crucial aspect of the humble argument is that it retains the vagueness of the vernacular use of the word God—a use that in Peirce's view best fits with our principal religious purposes (CP6.494). The trouble with the arguments of most theologians is that they seek to make their conception of God too precise. This introduces two problems: it inevitably changes the meaning of the word, and it is more easily shown to be unwarranted. For instance, in contrast to the popular notion of God as an omniscient, all powerful, and entirely benevolent Being, the vague, vernacular conception of God is not at all susceptible to a clever question like whether God can create a stone so heavy that He cannot lift it—a question that trades on what it means to be all-powerful. Our instinctive beliefs involving vague vernacular concepts, such as the concept of God, Peirce argues, "are far more trustworthy than the best established results of science, if these be precisely understood" (CP6.496). Not only is a vague belief more likely to be true, it is also more difficult to doubt, and as noted in the case of a belief in God a vague idea is really all we need. Peirce's neglected argument is also consistent with his conceptions of mind and self, as it has a decidedly behavioristic air to it: "we cannot tell what God would do, nor penetrate his counsels. We see what He *does* do, and nothing more" (CP6.613). For this reason, "one cannot logically infer the existence of God; one can only know Him by direct perception" (id.).

Earlier we saw that Peirce distinguishes three types of basic arguments: abduction, deduction, and induction (Section 4.3). The neglected argument, which draws a hypothesis from a great variety of qualitatively different observations, is a clear case of abduction. (Peirce also perceives perception as an unconscious form of abduction.) As abduction can be applied even to processes that are not controlled by a self, it can be applied also to musement, which as pure play is only barely self-controlled. Peirce further argues that just as birds have an instinct for building nests, we have an instinct for guessing things right. In Peirce's view, Kepler's discovery of the orbit of Mars and Galileo's discovery of the laws of dynamics show that we have such an instinct. In fact, without an instinct for guessing things right, we would be wholly at a loss when trying to extract the right answer from the endless sea of possibilities that presents itself in response to any question; that is to say, without such an instinct, we have "no chance of understanding nature, at all" (EP2:444). However, if we have an instinct for solving concrete questions like that of the orbit of Mars, it makes sense to say that this also applies to us choosing the hypothesis of God, especially when God is conceived in its vague, vernacular sense. In other words, because "we have an instinct for that which is rational," the force of the humble argument—though it "rests on far too many premises to be stated in full"—can be felt by every mind (R842:12–14). And, Peirce adds with confidence, this force will be felt by any mind once musement carries it far enough.

Now if we look at the neglected argument from the perspective of science, we come to see it as the first stage in a scientific inquiry that gives us "a hypothesis of the very highest Plausibility, whose ultimate test must lie in its value in the self-controlled growth of man's conduct of life" (EP2:446). It is possible to follow up on this stage with deduction to draw out testable consequences, and induction to actually test these consequences. In fact, Peirce approvingly cites a proposal he attributes to Tyndall to test the efficacy of prayer on the weather (R1287:3–6).

As for the reconciliation of science and religion it is not difficult to see where it goes. The best way to worship God is not by clinging tenaciously to some outmoded creed, but to inquire into reality with the genuine desire to discover how things truly are—as in that way we contribute to the growth of concrete reasonableness. The demand for right reasoning is thus not merely an esthetic and ethical one (Section 4.1), but is also a religious demand. Peirce's evolutionary cosmology sketched above can be seen as one attempt to flesh out the vague conception of God that the Humble Argument entitles us to believe in.

However, it is not just that religion should be scientific. Science should be conducted with a religious attitude as well. The genuine scientific inquirer, Peirce argues, has a loving admiration for nature not unlike that of religious devotion. The scientific inquirer, writes Peirce, "has an imperative need of finding in nature an object to love. His science cannot subsist without it" (R1334:21). A genuine desire to know can only be guided by a profound respect for its subject matter. Without it, science is quickly reduced to a technic subservient to practical problems. To underscore the importance of a religious disposition to science, Peirce advocates a "religion of science" (CP6.433). In a letter to Victoria Lady Welby he even goes so far as to say that despite the proclaimed atheism of many scientists, *scientific inquiry itself* presupposes a belief in God: "Every true man of science, i.e. every man belonging to a special group all the members of which sacrifice all the ordinary motives of life to their desire to make their beliefs concerning one subject conform to verified judgments of perception together with sound reasoning, and who therefore really believes the universe to be governed by reason, or in other words by God" (SS:75). The charge is not unlike the one cited in the previous chapter, that deep down scientists are realists, even though many fancy themselves to be nominalists. Moreover, just as we can say that a scientist who claims to have no metaphysics is at risk of falling victim to a very crude metaphysics, the scientist who claims to be a-religious is at risk of falling into a crude atheism. And as it turns out, nominalism and atheism often go hand in hand.

Peirce's argument, finally, is an argument for the *reality* of God, not for the *existence* of God. In fact, Peirce vehemently denies that God exists, stating that the proposition that He exists contains a contradiction in terms (R641:21). This brings us back to Peirce's distinction between reality and existence, which is discussed in Chapter 8. For Peirce, something is real when it is independent of what you or I or anyone in particular thinks it to be. Existence is one way in which something can be real. It is that mode of being, "which consists in [a] genuine dyadic relation of a strict individual with all the other such individuals" (CP6.336). This means that to say that God exists is to say that he reacts with other like things in the environment (CP6.495). Put differently, to say that God exists is to make Him into an existing *thing*, something on a par with rocks, tornados, and trees, and in Peirce's view this would be no less than an old-fashioned fetishism (id.). So almost in exact opposition to St Anselm—who argued that a Being than which no greater can be conceived must *ipso facto* exist—Peirce argues that God is a being whose very essence implies that He *cannot* exist. God is real, but he does not exist.

NOTES

Chapter 1

1. Murray Murphey takes this approach in *The Development of Peirce's Philosophy* (Cambridge, 1961).
2. Robert Crease "Charles Sanders Peirce and the first absolute measurement standard," *Physics Today* (December 2009): 29–44, p. 39.
3. Whitehead called Peirce the American Aristotle in a letter to Charles Hartshorne. Paul Weiss in his *Dictionary of American Biography* article on Peirce called him the American Leibniz.
4. For example, Edward Hogan *Of the Human Heart: A Biography of Benjamin Peirce* (Cranbury, 2008), and Bernard Cohen (ed.), *Benjamin Peirce: "Father of Pure Mathematics" in America* (New York, 1980).
5. Raymie E. McKerrow, "Richard Whately and the revival of logic in nineteenth-century England," *Rhetorica* 5.2 (1987): 163–85.
6. Whately's *Elements of Logic*, Introduction, section 5.
7. Letter of Charles Peirce to F.A. Woods, October 14, 1913.
8. George Whalley, "Coleridge and the self-unraveling clue," In H.J. Jackson (ed.), *Editing Polymaths: Erasmus to Russell* (Toronto, 1983), pp. 17–40; quotation from p. 20.
9. William James, *Pragmatism: A New Name for Some Old Ways of Thinking* (New York, 1907), p. 2.
10. Carl Bode and Malcolm Cowley (eds), *The Portable Emerson* (New York, 1981), p. 57.
11. Ian Hacking, *Representing and Intervening* (Cambridge, 1983), p. 61.
12. Joseph Brent's *Charles S. Peirce: A Life* (Bloomington, 1998) is the only full biography in the English language, but it fails to connect Peirce's life with his work and irresponsibly ascribes to Peirce personal and mental problems for which there is little or no evidence.
13. See especially Nathan Houser, "The Fortunes and Misfortunes of the Peirce Papers," in *Signs of Humanity,* edited by Michel Balat and Janice Deledalle-Rhodes (Berlin, 1992) 3: 1259–68.

14 Martin Heidegger, *Holtzwege* (Frankfurt am Main, 1950), p. 3.
15 "Traditions of innovation & improvisation: jazz as metaphor, philosophy as jazz," in Cornelis de Waal and Krzysztof Skowroński (eds), *The Normative Philosophy of Charles Peirce* (New York, 2012), p. 5.

Chapter 2

1 Cited by Paul Weiss in his entry on Peirce in the *Dictionary of American Biography* (1934).
2 Carolyn Eisele in vol. 2 of her *New Elements of Mathematics* has since published both, albeit out of chronological order.
3 *Critique of Pure Reason*, A711/B739.
4 *Critique of Pure Reason*, A 716/B744; the proof is found in Euclid's *Elements*, and is no doubt older than that. It relies heavily on Euclid's parallel postulate so that the space of Kant's pure intuition is in effect Euclidean space.
5 Kant does not deny the possibility of applied mathematics. See A726/B754.
6 Cantor, George, *Grundlagen einer allgemeinen Manigfaltigkeitslehre* (Leipzig, 1883), section 8.
7 Benjamin Peirce, *Linear Associative Algebra* (Washington, 1870), section 1; Charles Peirce edited a new edition of this work in 1882, published by Van Nostrand, New York.
8 Ibid.
9 In the *Century Dictionary* Peirce defines mathematics as: "the study of ideal construction (often applicable to real problems), and the discovery thereby of relations between the parts of these constructions, before unknown" (CD:3659).
10 Joseph Jastrow. "The mind's eye." *Popular Science Monthly* 54 (1899): 299–312, p. 312. Jastrow was a student of Peirce at Johns Hopkins.
11 Letter to James Mills Peirce, 18 November 1894.

Chapter 3

1 Note that the prominence given to the term phenomenology in the *Collected Papers* is due to the editors.
2 William James, *Pragmatism: A New Name for Some Old Ways of Thinking* (New York, 1908), p. 172.

3 William James, *Principles of Psychology* (New York, 1890), 1: 488.
4 Note that for James fancies too are "in their first intention mere bits of pure experience" (*Essays in Radical Empiricism* [New York, 1912], p. 15).
5 John Locke, *An Essay Concerning Human Understanding*, edited by Peter Nidditch (Oxford, 1975), I.i.8.
6 On 22 July 1902 this causes Peirce to writes in his "Logic Notebook": "the doctrine of the categories must precede mathematics" (R339).
7 The phrase "to realize" recalls Kant's notion of construction (Section 2.1).
8 I am making a slight modification to Peirce's original example (which can be found at CP8.330), suggested to me by Ivan Mladinov.
9 Charles S. Peirce, "Pythagorics," *The Open Court* No. 263 (8 September 1892): 3375–77, p. 3376.

Chapter 4

1 Peirce also connects them with the three categories in their psychological aspect: feeling, reaction, and thought (CP8.256).
2 In CP2.208, Peirce identifies eight different sources for distinguishing good from bad reasoning, and in the subsequent paragraphs he discusses each of them.
3 A psychologistic logic also requires logicians to revisit their theories every time there is a major shift in psychology.
4 Peirce agrees, though, that we can learn much from studying how people have successfully argued in the past and from the mistakes that were made, and he wrote and lectured extensively on the history of scientific reasoning.
5 CD:2011, entry for esthetic ($2n1$); Peirce did not write the entry for esthetics.
6 CD:78; interleaf addition. Peirce gives the example of admiring a woman's dress.
7 In his interleaved copy, Peirce corrected the definition for *deduction* by replacing "from a known principle" with "of assumed principles." He apparently forgot to make the same correction for his definition of the verb *to deduce*, which is therefore put into square brackets.
8 For Peirce's definition of mathematical induction, see CD:3068.

9   Letter to J. H. Kehler, 22 June 1911.
10 Abduction is defined in a way not altogether unlike Peirce, for instance, in William Fleming's *Vocabulary of Philosophy* (Philadelphia, 1860), which clearly antedates the *Century Dictionary*. This third mode was first proposed by Aristotle, *Posterior Analytics*, Bk. 2, section 25.
11 For example, Peter Lipton, "Inference to the best explanation," in W. H. Newton-Smith (ed.), *A Companion to the Philosophy of Science* (Oxford, 2000): 184–93, especially p. 184.
12 Letter to Paul Carus, possibly end of August 1910 (RL77:230f).
13 Said during an address given in 1922; published in *Selected Works*, ed. L. Borkowski (Amsterdam, 1970), p. 111.
14 W. V. O. Quine, "In the logical vestibule," *Times Literary Supplement* 12 (1985), p. 767.
15 W. V. O. Quine, "Peirce's logic," in Kenneth L. Ketner (ed.), *Peirce and Contemporary Thought* (New York, 1995), pp. 23–31; see p. 24.
16 Before Peirce, Leonard Euler and John Venn used circle diagrams to treat the logic of classes.
17 Letter to Philip Jourdain, 5 December 1908.
18 In 1964, Jay Zeman showed that with minimal modifications to its rules the gamma graphs can be made isomorphic with the well-known modal logics S4 and S5. See *The Graphical Logic of C. S. Peirce* (Doctoral Dissertation, University of Chicago, 1964). For C. I. Lewis's modal logics (S1–S5), see C. I. Lewis and C. H. Langford, *Symbolic Logic* (New York, 1932).
19 This is why Peirce calls it the *existential* graphs; inscribing something on the sheet of assertion means that it *exists* in the universe which that sheet represents. For the same reason he calls it elsewhere a *positive* system of logic (see R488:2).
20 An accessible account of these rules is found in Don Roberts, *The existential graphs of Charles S. Peirce* (The Hague, 1973), Ch. 3, and in Kenneth L. Ketner, *Elements of Logic: An Introduction to Peirce's Existential Graphs* (Lubbock, 1990), Ch. 3. Note that Peirce's rules are pragmatic; they are "*permissions* to do certain things under expressed general circumstances" (R280:24).

Chapter 5

1   *An Essay Concerning Human Understanding* (Oxford, 1975), IV.xxiii.4.
2   Op. cit.

3 *An Investigation of the Laws of Thought* (London, 1854).
4 Letter to Charles A. Strong, 25 July 1904.
5 Peirce did not write the entry for semeiotics in the *Century Dictionary*, though he marked it in his personal copy as one he worked on. The exact same definition appears in the *Imperial Dictionary*, for which the Century Company had bought the rights and which formed the basis for the *Century Dictionary*. The *Century Dictionary* has an entry for *semeiology:* "The logical theory of signs, of the conditions of their fulfilling their functions, of their chief kinds, etc." Though Peirce did not mark it, it is suspected that he wrote this entry, which is not in the *Imperial*.
6 Robert Innis, *Semiotics: An Introductory Anthology* (Bloomington, 1985), p. 40.
7 Op. cit., 43.
8 See, for example, Benson Mates, *Stoic Logic* (Berkeley, 1953), chapter 2.
9 Some of Peirce's equivalent terms for rheme are rhematic sign and seme, for dicent he also uses dicisign and pheme, and for argument he also uses delome.

Chapter 6

1 Mozert v. Hawkins County Public Schools, United States Court of Appeals, Sixth Circuit.
2 Karl Popper, *Conjectures and Refutations* (London, 1972), pp. 34–9.
3 *Critique of Pure Reason,* B:xl.
4 Letter to Cassius J. Keyser, October 1,1907.

Chapter 7

1 See John J. McDermott (ed.), *The Writings of William James* (Chicago, 1967), p. 348.
2 See, for example, Cornelis de Waal, *On Pragmatism* (Belmont, 2005).
3 Ralph B. Perry, *The Thought and Character of William James* (Boston, 1935), 2: 409.
4 Undated letter to William James written *c.*1908.
5 Letter to Paul Carus, 19 July 1910; emphasis added.

6   Letter to F. W. Frankland, 25 February 1907.
7   Letter to Christine Ladd Franklin, 28 October 1904.
8   V. W. O. Quine, *From a Logical Point of View* 2nd edn. (Cambridge, Mass., 1980), p. 37.
9   Ludwig Wittgenstein, *Philosophical Investigations*, 2nd edn. (Oxford, 1958), section 43.
10 Robert M. Young, *Excursions in Calculus* (Washington DC, 1992), p. 417.
11 Letter to C. A. Strong, 25 July 1904.

Chapter 8

1   *Oxford English Dictionary* (online edn), accessed 16 February 2012.
2   For sake of the argument, I am assuming that the conclusion is true; that is, that it would be agreed upon "at the end of inquiry."

Chapter 9

1   Letter to Charles A. Strong, 25 July 1904.
2   "Catastrophism and evolution," *American Naturalist* 11 (1877): 449–70.
3   Peirce contrasts hyperbolic evolution, or movement, with what he sees as the only two other options, elliptic movement and parabolic movement, neither of which is truly evolutionary (W6:392). The three correspond respectively to the Epicurean, pessimist and evolutionist view in the first chapter of *A Guess at the Riddle* (W6:174).
4   For a good example of the traditional view see Locke's *Essay*, Book III.
5   Xenophon, Memorabilia I.4.6.
6   William Paley, *Natural Theology: or, Evidences of the Existence and Attributes of the Deity* (London, 1803), Chapter 3.
7   Letter to James McKeen Cattell, 26 January 1906.
8   Letter to William James, 25 December 1909.
9   Letter to William James, 25 December 1909.
10 Thomas Aquinas, *Summa Theologica*, Part I, Question 2, Article 3.

BIBLIOGRAPHY

The bibliography below is highly selective and not meant to be more than a first introduction to the literature, which is varied and extensive. Bibliographic information on primary sources used is given at the beginning of this volume (see *Abbreviations*).

Anderson, Douglas. *Strands of System: The Philosophy of Charles Peirce.* West Lafayette, IN: Purdue University Press, 1995.

Apel, Karl-Otto. *Charles S. Peirce: From Pragmatism to Pragmaticism.* Amherst, MA: University of Massachusetts Press, 1981.

Bernstein, Richard. *Perspectives on Peirce: Critical Essays on Charles Sanders Peirce.* New Haven: Yale University Press, 1965.

Boler, John. *Charles Peirce and Scholastic Realism.* Seattle: University of Washington Press, 1963.

Brent, Joseph. *Charles Sanders Peirce: A Life* (2nd edn). Bloomington, IN: Indiana University Press, 1993.

Brunning, Jacqueline and Paul Forster. *The Rule of Reason: The philosophy of Charles Sanders Peirce.* Toronto: University of Toronto Press, 1997.

Buchler, Justus. *Charles Peirce's Empiricism.* New York: Harcourt, 1939.

Colapietro, Vincent. *Peirce's Approach to the Self.* Albany, NY: State University of New York Press, 1989.

de Waal, Cornelis. *On Peirce.* Belmont, CA: Wadsworth, 2001.

de Waal, Cornelis and Krzysztof Skowroński (eds). *The Normative Thought of Charles S. Peirce.* New York: Fordham, 2012.

Debrock, Guy and Menno Hulswit. *Living Doubt: Essays Concerning the Epistemology of Charles Sanders Peirce.* Dordrecht: Kluwer Academic Publishers, 1994.

Delaney, Cornelius. *Science, Knowledge, and Mind: A Study in the Philosophy of C. S. Peirce.* Notre Dame, IN: University of Notre Dame Press, 1993.

Eisele, Carolyn. *Studies in the Scientific and Mathematical Philosophy of Charles S. Peirce.* R. M. Martin (ed.). The Hague: Mouton, 1979.

Fisch, Max. *Peirce, Semeiotic, and Pragmatism*. Kenneth Ketner and Christian Kloesel (eds). Bloomington, IN: Indiana University Press, 1986.
Forster, Paul. *Peirce and the Threat of Nominalism*. Cambridge: Cambridge University Press, 2011.
Freeman, Eugene (ed.). *The Relevance of Charles Peirce*. La Salle, IL: Monist Library of Philosophy, 1983.
Hausman, Carl. *Charles S. Peirce's Evolutionary Philosophy*. Cambridge: Cambridge University Press, 1993.
Hookway, Christopher. *Peirce*. London: Routledge, 1985.
—*Truth, Rationality, and Pragmatism: Themes from Peirce*. Oxford: Oxford University Press, 2000.
Houser, Nathan, Don Roberts, and James Van Evra. *Studies in the Logic of Charles Sanders Peirce*. Bloomington, IN: Indiana University Press, 1997.
Kent, Beverly. *Charles S. Peirce: Logic and the Classification of the Sciences*. Kingston: McGill-Queen's University Press, 1987.
Ketner, Kenneth (ed.). *Peirce and Contemporary Thought*. New York: Fordham University Press, 1995.
Ketner, Kenneth, Christian Kloesel, and Joseph Ransdell (eds). *A Comprehensive Bibliography and Index of the Published Works of Charles Sanders Peirce* (2nd edn). Bowling Green: Philosophy Documentation Center, 1986.
Liszka, James. *A General Introduction to the Semeiotic of Charles Sanders Peirce*. Bloomington: Indiana University Press, 1996.
Mayorga, Rosa. *From Realism to "Realicism": The Metaphysics of Charles Sanders Peirce*. Lanham, MD: Lexington Books, 2007.
Misak, Cheryl. *Truth and the End of Inquiry* (2nd edn). Oxford: Oxford University Press, 2004.
—(ed.). *The Cambridge Companion to Peirce*. Cambridge: Cambridge University Press, 2004.
Moore, Edward and Richard Robin (eds). *Studies in the Philosophy of Charles Sanders Peirce*. Amherst, MA: University of Massachusetts Press, 1964.
—*From Time and Chance to Consciousness: Studies in the Metaphysics of Charles Peirce*. New York: State University of New York Press, 1994.
Moore, Matthew (ed.). *New Essays on Peirce's Mathematical Philosophy*. Chicago: Open Court Publishing, 2010.
Mounce, H. *The Two Pragmatisms: From Peirce to Rorty*. New York: Routledge, 1997.
Murphy, Murray. *The Development of Peirce's Philosophy*. Cambridge: Harvard University Press, 1961.
Oleksy, Mateusz. *Realism and Individualism: Charles S. Peirce and the Threat of Modern Nominalism*. Lodz: Lodz University Press, 2008.

Parker, Kelly. *The Continuity of Peirce's Thought*. Nashville, TN: Vanderbilt University Press, 1998.

Peirce, Charles. *Historical perspectives on Peirce's Logic of Science*. 2 vols. Carolyn Eisele (ed.). Amsterdam: Mouton, 1985.

—*Pragmatism as a Principle and Method of Right Thinking*. Patricia Turrisi (ed.). Albany, NY: State University of New York Press, 1997.

Pietarinen, Ahti–Veikko. *Signs of Logic: Peircean Themes on the Philosophy of Language, Games, and Communication*. Dordrecht: Springer, 2006.

Potter, Vincent. *Charles S. Peirce: On Norms and Ideals*. Worcester. MA: University of Massachusetts, 1967.

Raposa, Michael. *Peirce's Philosophy of Religion*. Bloomington, IN: Indiana University Press, 1989.

Rescher, Nicholas. *Peirce's Philosophy of Science*. Notre Dame, IN: University of Notre Dame Press, 1978.

Reynolds, Andrew. *Peirce's Scientific Metaphysics*. Nashville, TN: Vanderbilt University Press, 2002.

Roberts, Don. *The Existential Graphs of Charles S. Peirce*. The Hague: Mouton, 1973.

Rosenthal, Sandra. *Charles Peirce's Pragmatic Pluralism*. Albany, NY: State University of New York Press, 1994.

Shin, Sun-Joo. *The Iconic Logic of Peirce's Graphs*. Cambridge, MA: MIT Press, 2002.

Short, Thomas L. *Peirce's Theory of Signs*. Cambridge: Cambridge University Press, 2007.

Transactions of the Charles S. Peirce Society. A quarterly journal dedicated to the work of Peirce and American philosophy more generally. 1965–.

INDEX

a priori method 97f
abduction 50, 71
  defined 63, 168
  justification of 65
  and the neglected
    argument 162
  as part of scientific
    reasoning 65f, 105
  and pragmatism 119
abstraction
  hypostatic 28, 67, 89
  prescissive and hypostatic
    distinguished 27
actuality 128
agapism 148
algebra
  dichotomic 31
  logical 29
alpha graphs, defined 71
analytic-synthetic distinction 120
anancism 147
Anselm of Canterbury 164
anthethics 51
anthropomorphism 135
anti-cock-sure-ism 94
Aquinas, Thomas 160
argument 57, 89, 117
  vs argumentation 160
Aristotle 13, 45, 54, 121
  abduction 168
  categories 37, 46
arithmetic 30
assertion 71
  sheet of 71

authority, method of 96f
axiagastics 53

Bain, Alexander 109
Barringer Crater 100, 102
Barringer, Daniel 100
beauty 48, 51, 53
being 45
belief
  Bain's definition 109
  defined 95f
  fixation of 57, 94–101
  vs habit 95
Bentham, Jeremy 34
Berkeley, George 137, 139
beta graphs, defined 71
Bolyai, János 143
Boole, George 5, 29
  calculus of classes 69
  semeiotics 73
Boyle, Robert 115
Brahe, Tycho 63
brain-in-a-vat hypothesis,
  pragmatism applied to 121
British empiricists 36
buried secrets 134
Burks, Arthur 9

Calderoni, Mario 110
Cantor, Georg 20
Carnap, Rudolf 119
Cartesianism, critique of 78
Carus, Paul 115, 132
categorics 35, 37

INDEX

categories
  cenopythagorean 46
  derivation of 39
  doctrine of 37, 152
  Protean 46
  universal vs particular 39
Cattell, James McKeen 158
causality 88
cenoscopy 34
chance 150
  doctrine of 149
  evolution a product of 146
  no purely epistemic
    notion 144
class, defined 59
classification
  natural vs artificial 10
  of the sciences 10–12
  of signs 90–3
clearness, three grades of 111f, 121
Colapietro, Vincent 8
Coleridge, Samuel Taylor 106
collateral experience 86
Comte, August 11–12, 15
concrete reasonableness
  155–7, 159
  defined 156
conjecture and refutation 106
consciousness *see also* mind
  belief 95
  interpretant 82f
  phaneron 35
consequentiae, doctrine of 59
construction 27f, 166
  of concepts 18f
continuity, doctrine of 149, 151
  see also synechism
  true 30
convention 88
Cook, James 9
Coriolis, Gaspard 51
cosmology 145
  evolutionary 145, 148,
    158, 163

counterfactual conditionals 134
Crease, Robert 3
critic 56, 74
critical common-sensism 94, 157

da Vinci, Leonardo 3
Darwin, Charles 54, 91, 94, 157
De Morgan, Augustus 69
Dedekind, Richard 29
deduction 60
  corollarial vs
    theorematic 26, 61
  defined 25, 60
  as part of scientific
    reasoning 65f, 105
definition, abstract 112
  pragmatistic 112f
degenerate cases 28, 44
delome 169
Descartes, René 93, 95, 97
  evil-demon argument 121
  method of doubt 94
  mind 54, 153
  reasoning 104
determinism 132
  critique of 142–4
Dewey, John 110
dicent 89
dicisign 169
discrimination 42
  defined 39
dissociation 42
  defined 39
doubt, method of 94f
Duns Scotus 127f

economy of research 119
  belongs to speculative
    rhetoric 57, 105
  theory of 86
Eisele, Carolyn 9
Eliot, Charles H. 5, 7
Emerson, Ralph Waldo 7
Empedocles 148

INDEX

ens rationis 27f, 42, 80
ens realis 67, 80
epistemic agnosticism 95
error 102, 153
   the self defined in
      terms of 157
esthetics
   beauty 51, 53
   defined 35, 51f
   ideal of 53
   science of discovery 47
ethics
   defined 35, 51
   science of discovery 47
   theoretical science 50
Euclid 72, 143
   Elements 16, 28, 142, 166
Euler, Leonard 168
evil-demon argument, pragmatism
      applied to 121
evolution *see also* agapism;
      anancism; tychism
   by creative love 148
   Darwinian 146
   hyperbolic 148, 170
   Kingean 146
   Lamarckian 146
   metaphysical conception
      of 146
existence 128, 149
   in the graphs 168
experimentation, voluntary 103
explanation; defined 145
externalism 151 *see also* mind

fallibilism 61, 94, 106
falsifiability 106, 119
feeling 152, 159
firstness 46, 145f
   in cosmology 149
   defined 41
   as a phaneroscopic category 43
Fisch, Max H. 9
Fiske, John 109

four-color theorem 128
freedom 150
Frege, Gottlob 69
Frost, Vicki 96

Galileo 13, 97, 162
gamma graphs
   defined 71
   isomorphic with
      modal logic 168
generalization 23, 38
   the true engine of
      mathematics 28
geometrical optics *see* projective
      geometry
geometry
   non-Euclidean 15, 22, 28, 142
   projective 70
   topical 30, 70
Gilbert, Grove Karl 100
God 158 *see also* neglected
      argument
   defined 160
   reality and non-existence
      of 163
   vernacular conception of 161
graphics 70 *see also* projective
      geometry
graphs *see also* alpha graph; beta
      graph; gamma graph
   existential 5, 69–72, 168
   governed by pragmatic
      rules 168
   method of 40
   a positive system of logic 168
   second intentional 71
   used to represent abduction and
      induction 71
Green, Nicholas St John 109
Grosseteste, Robert 98

habit 95, 115, 161 *see also*
      natural law
   in Lamarckian evolution 147

Hacking, Ian 7
hardness, pragmatism
  applied to 123
Hart, James 73
Hartmann, Eduard 152
Hartshorne, Charles 8
Hegel, Georg W. F. 36
  categories 46, 97
Heidegger, Martin 8
heuretic science 11f
Hjelmslev, Louis 76f
Holmes, Oliver W. 109
Horsford, Eben 4
humble argument for the reality
  of God 161, 163 see also
  neglected argument
hypothesis see abduction

icon 88f, 114
idea
  abstract 5
  association of 50, 89, 118
  defined 111
  defined (Locke) 36
idealism 101, 139 see also
  objective idealism
  conditional 139
idioscopy 34
ignorance 102, 153
  the self defined in
    terms of 157
imaginary numbers 22
imagination 23
  mathematical 22
incommensurables, pragmatism
  applied to 122
index 88f
induction 60, 71
  defined 61
  justification of 62
  mathematical 61, 167
  as part of scientific
    reasoning 65f, 105

qualitative, quantitative, or
  crude 66
self-correcting 62
inference to the best explanation 65
inquiry 93
  communal affair 57
instinct 126
  and abduction 119, 162
  vs reason 53f
interpretant 79, 81, 153
  dynamic 83f, 88, 113
  emotional 84
  energetic 85
  final 83f, 113, 131
  immediate 83f, 131
  intended 84
  logical 85
  potential 80
  ultimate 83f
intuition 15, 126
  pure 18–19
inverse square law 151
it, the 37

James, William 7, 109f, 159
  interpretation of
    pragmatism 123
  pure experience 36, 167
Jastrow, Joseph 26
Jesus, a pragmatist 110
Jourdain, Philip 79

Kant, Immanuel 6, 97f, 135
  categorical imperative 53
  categories 45f
  conception of
    mathematics 17–20
  logic 45, 56, 67
  notion of construction
    18f, 167
  things in themselves 122
Kehler, J. H. 116
Kepler, Johannes 63f, 162

Kernan, W. Fergus 8
Ketner, Kenneth L. 9
Keyser, Cassius J. 105
King, Clarence 146f
Kirchheiss, Johannes 14, 108, 140
Kondo, Shigeru 122

Lamarck, Jean-Baptiste 147
langue 77
Lavoisier, Antoine 56, 103
leading principle
   defined 57
   habit of reasoning 58
   material vs logical 59
   truth of 59
legisign 88
Lewis, C. I. 110
Liebig, Justus 4
Liebig's method 4
light of nature 156
linear perspective, doctrine of 70
Lipton, Peter 168
Lobachevski, Nikolai 143
Locke, John 5, 56
   his notion of idea 36
   influence on Whately and Boole 73
   on logic and semeiotics 73
logic 13, 126 *see also* semeiotics
   algebra of 29
   Aristotelian 69
   defined 34
   emotivist approach to 49
   formal semiotic 80
   mathematical 49, 69
   non-relative 31
   a normative science 47, 53
   a positive science 29, 49
   theory of deliberate thinking 50
   three-valued 69
logica docens 116
   defined 55f

logica utens 116
   defined 55–7
   and induction 61
   and leading principles 58
   musement 160
Logical Empiricists 119f
logicism 29, 31
logic of relations *see* logic of relatives
logic of relatives 66f, 69, 79
long run, conception of 59, 61f, 130, 149, 157f
love
   Christian 148
   creative 147
Lukasiewicz, Jan 69

man-sign 154
   doctrine of 78
Marquand, Alan 2
Mars, orbit of 63f, 162
mathematician, three powers of 22
mathematics 12, 15
   axioms of 142, 144
   defined 20f, 23, 166
   division of 30
   not reducible to demonstration 28
   observation and experiment crucial 24
   Platonism 129
Mead, George H. 110
Metaphysical Club 109f
metaphysics 34, 141, 148
   definition of 125
   general, physical, or psychical 127, 141
   Kantian notion of 157
   a positive science 143
   relation to mathematics 142
methodeutic *see* speculative grammar

mind 150–3, 155, 162
   dialogic conception of 152f
   externalist view of 151, 154
   semeiotic conception of 82, 153f
   unconscious 152
misinterpretation 84
Mladinov, Ivan 167
modality 71
modal logics 168
Morris, Charles W. 74
multiple personality disorder 154
musement 160
   form of abduction 162

natural law 145, 148
   emerge as habits 150
   real 128, 137
natural light 156
necessitarianism 142 *see also* determinism
neglected argument for the reality of God 161 *see also* humble argument
Newcomb, Simon 7
Newton, Isaac 151
nominalism 48, 123, 136
normative science 34
   part of mathematics 48
Norris, Howes 115

object 79, 85, 153
   dynamic 86–8, 131
   immediate 86, 88
objective idealism 101, 122, 139, 151

Paley, William 155f, 158
Papini, Giovanni 110
parallel postulate 143, 166
parole 77
Peirce, Benjamin 1, 3–5, 21
Peirce, Charles Henry 4

Peirce, Charles Sanders
   a scientist 6, 93, 98, 100, 136
   upbringing 3–6
Peirce's law 69
Peirce's theorem 42
periodic table 91
Perry, Ralph B. 110
personal identity 154
personhood 154f
person vs mind 150
phaneron 36, 46, 111
   defined 35
   indecomposable parts of 40
   ingredients of 37, 39
phaneroscopy *see* phenomenology
pheme 169
phenomenon 12, 35f, 48, 98, 127, 138
   brought about by scientists 115
phenomenology 34
   defined 51
   three faculties needed 38
philosophy 33, 111, 125
   dependent upon mathematical reasoning 16, 29
   division of 12, 34
   a positive science 12, 18, 33f
philosophy of science; belongs to speculative rhetoric 57
Plato 13
play 160, 162
pleasure 52
Popper, Sir Karl 96, 106, 119
positive science 12, 15, 18
   defined 33
   relation to normative science 47
positivism 12, 126
possibility
   pure 149
   real 123, 131, 137
Post, Emil 69
potentiality 150, 159

INDEX

pragmatic maxim 109, 115
  applications of 120
  defined 112
  a normative principle 119
  vs verification principle 120, 122
pragmaticism 111
pragmatics 74
pragmatism 101, 161
  belongs to speculative rhetoric 57
  defined 116
  the logic of abduction 65, 119
  a maxim of logic 116
  origin 109
  proof of 116f
prayer, efficacy of 162
prescission 27, 42 *see also* abstraction
  defined 39
presumption 63 *see also* abduction
Prezzolini, Giuseppe 110
Principia Mathematica 69
Proteus 46
psychologism 49, 80f
pure experience, James' notion of 36
Pythagorean decad 46
Pythagoreanism 29, 46

qualisign 88
quantification theory 69
quasi mind 82
Quine, W. V. O. 69

realism 48, 123, 136f
  extreme scholastic 125, 139
  perceptual 139
reality 101
  abstractly defined 127
  pragmatically defined 130

reason, first rule of 105
  naturalistic account of 54
reasonableness *see also* concrete reasonableness
  development of 115
  an esthetic ideal 52
  of the universe 156
reasoning
  chain vs rope 104, 117
  defined 57, 96
  diagrammatic 17, 23, 29
  distinguishing good from bad 167
  habits of 114
  mathematical 16f, 23, 61
  philosophical 17
  scientific 65
relation, dyadic or polyadic 68
  see also logic of relatives
relative 67
  triadic 68
religion 158 *see also* science
replica 88
representamen 78 *see also* sign
resemblance 88
retroduction 60 *see also* abduction
rheme 89
rhetoric 57
Riemann, Bernhard 143
rigid body, idea of 70 *see also* metrics
Robin, Richard 9
Royce, Josiah 2, 8
Russell, Bertrand 37, 69

Saussure, Ferdinand 75f, 79
Schiller, Ferdinand 110
  notion of *Spiel-Trieb* 160
Schiller, Friedrich 6
science
  defined 98f
  definition of 11, 106

method of 96, 98–9, 101–2
nominalistic or realistic 137, 163
and religion 163
social nature of 102
scientific attitude 104
scientific metaphysics 12, 126, 144
scientific method 11, 103f
secondness 46, 145f
   in cosmology 149
   defined 41
   degenerate 44
   as a phaneroscopic category 43
self 162
   defined 102, 157
self-control 50, 114, 119, 133, 150, 162
self-correction thesis 62
self-identity 82
semeiosis 78
   thought a process of 153
   unlimited 82
semeiotics 131, 169 *see also* logic; speculative grammar
   defined 74
   early seeds of 5
   Locke's notion of 73
   relation to logic 57, 74, 117
semeiology 169
semiology 75
semiotics 75
sense data 37
separation, grades of 39
Shakespeare, William 127
sham reasoning 158
Sheffer, Henry 69
Sheffer stroke 69
Shelley, Mary 102
Shoemaker, Eugene 100
sign
   arbitrary (Saussure) 76
   defined 78–80, 117

   natural 76
   and thought 153
   triadic 79
sign action 153
signifier-signified 76f, 79
Sigwart, Christoph 49
sinsign 88
Snell, Willebrord 98
Socrates 155
speculative grammar 56f, 74
   identified with semeiotics 57, 74
speculative rhetoric 56f, 74, 105, 124
Spencer, Herbert 11, 122, 147
Spinoza, Baruch 16
spontaneity 149f
statistical mechanics 151
Stevenson, Louis 102
Stöckhardt, Julius A. 4
Strong, Charles A. 124
substance 37, 45f
summum bonum 157
Sylvester, James J. 16
symbol 88f
synechism 148f
   belongs to speculative rhetoric 57, 105

tenacity, method of 96
terminology, ethics of 13
testability 119
things in themselves 122
thirdness 46, 145
   in cosmology 149
   defined 41
   degenerate 44, 146
   as a phaneroscopic category 43
thought 153–5 *see also* mind
token 87
tone 87

topology 70 *see also* geometry
transubstantiation, pragmatism
   applied to 120f
trichotomies 90
truth
   the aim of thought 50
   correspondence and coherence
      theories of 127
   pragmatic conception of
      101, 131
truth-functional analysis 69
truth table 69
tuone 88
tychism 141, 146
Tyndall 162
type 87

Überweg, Friedrich 47f
US Coast Survey 3, 6, 7

Vailati, Giovanni 110
Venn diagram 26
Venn, John 168
verification 119f, 122

Weiss, Paul 8
Weissman, August 147
Welby, Victoria Lady 79, 86, 163
Wittgenstein, Ludwig 120
Whalley, George 7
Whately, Richard 5
   semeiotics 73
Whitehead, Alfred North 69
will, the 82
Wright, Chauncey 109

Yee, Alexander 122

Zeman, Jay 168

www.ingramcontent.com/pod-product-compliance
Lightning Source LLC
Chambersburg PA
CBHW060954230426
43665CB00015B/2196